WHAT'S
YOUR
DECISION?

WHAT'S YOUR DECISION?

How to Make Choices with Confidence and Clarity

An Ignatian
Approach
to
Decision Making

J. MICHAEL SPAROUGH, SJ, JIM MANNEY, AND TIM HIPSKIND, SJ

LOYOLAPRESS.
A JESUIT MINISTRY
Chicago

LOYOLA PRESS.
A JESUIT MINISTRY

3441 N. Ashland Avenue
Chicago, Illinois 60657
(800) 621-1008
www.loyolapress.com

Cover design by Larry Cope, cope-design
Interior design by Megan Duffy Rostan and Joan Bledig

Library of Congress Cataloging-in-Publication Data
Sparough, J. Michael.
  What's your decision? : how to make choices with clarity and confidence : an Ignatian approach / J. Michael Sparough, Jim Manney, and Tim Hipskind.
      p. cm.
  ISBN-13: 978-0-8294-3148-3
  ISBN-10: 0-8294-3148-9
  1. Decision making—Religious aspects—Catholic Church. 2. Ignatius, of Loyola, Saint, 1491–1556. Exercitia spiritualia. I. Manney, Jim. II. Hipskind, Tim. III. Title.
  BV4509.5.S7 2010
  248.4'82—dc22

                                                                2009048401

Printed in the United States of America
15 16 17 18 19 20 Versa 10 9 8 7 6 5 4

For our Jesuit mentors,
who taught us these lessons
and lived their decisions in love.

CONTENTS

PREFACE

T his book is about making decisions. Many books, workshops, seminars, podcasts, and self-study programs give advice about personal development. But less attention is given to the actual process of making a sound decision. How do you go about choosing between plausible, attractive alternatives? What factors are most important? What do you do when your heart conflicts with your head? These are the problems we are interested in here.

The approach we take was first laid out almost five hundred years ago by Ignatius of Loyola, a towering figure in the history of spirituality. Ignatius's ideas about decision making and spiritual growth have had immense influence in the world—they have permeated the general secular culture. All those books and programs about personal development owe a debt to Ignatius's insights and to the spiritual tradition based on them.

You don't have to be a spiritual giant to make use of this book. Ignatius founded the Jesuits, the largest religious order in the Catholic Church, but he was a layman when he developed his approach to discernment and decision making. So he wrote for ordinary people. He was very observant, noticing what worked and what didn't. You don't have to be steeped in religious practice or have definitions of Christian doctrine at your fingertips to understand what he was saying.

You do need to accept a couple of principles. Chief among them is the conviction that God is active in your life and cares about your decisions. The Ignatian approach also calls for a couple of prerequisites: a sincere desire to choose the good and a willingness to do what's necessary to become free enough to make the best choice.

If you have the desire and are willing to do what's necessary, then you can make use of the soundest approach to decision making ever invented. Actually, Ignatius didn't invent anything; he discovered some things that are true. That's what this book is about.

CHAPTER 1

First Principles

When Wendy was a junior in high school, an epidemic of methamphetamine abuse swept through her small Ohio town. Several friends became addicted. One died in an auto accident caused by a driver high on meth. Many adults in the town became addicted and some lost their homes, businesses, and marriages. Several went to prison. Wendy knew people who tried and failed to break their addiction to this powerful drug. While still in high school, she resolved to do something about it.

The desire to help drug addicts grew while Wendy was in college. She graduated with honors and went to medical school. Now she is a resident in internal medicine, specializing in substance abuse. She likes working with addicts. She's impressed with new treatment approaches and wants to work as a physician in a drug and alcohol treatment facility. Such work doesn't pay well, but Wendy doesn't care about money. She wants to help addicts. Although she's not a regular churchgoer, she does believe that there is inherent meaning to life—it's not just a random set *of circumstances. She has felt the stirring of a sense of purpose while working in her chosen field, and she has found that prayerful reflection helps a lot in the process of choosing that work.*

Wendy is in love with Robert, who is finishing his MBA. Robert wants to make money. He's bright, energetic, and sought after by prospective employers. Now he is deciding among three attractive job offers: an analyst for a hedge fund, a position with a promising biotech start-up company, and a job with a multinational bank. Robert wants Wendy to marry him. He's generous and kind, and Wendy feels deeply for him, but he doesn't share her desire to help addicts. He's tried to convince Wendy to go into a more lucrative branch of medicine. His philosophy is "Let's get rich. Then we can do anything. We can start our own treatment clinic if that's what you want."

Wendy is torn. Sometimes Robert's attitude displeases her, but at other times, it makes sense. She loves Robert, but she realizes she would have to give up her vision of a future to marry him. What should she do?

GOD CARES ABOUT OUR DECISIONS

How should Wendy go about making this decision? That's what this book is about. Here we present a methodology for decision making that has helped millions of people make sound and satisfying choices. The first step is to lay out our assumptions. What do we need to believe to make a good decision?

The first premise is that God cares about our decisions. This isn't self-evident, and not everyone believes it. Many people don't want to believe it. The notion that a higher power outside themselves has a stake in the choices they make strikes them as an impingement on their freedom. Even believers often share this sentiment to some degree. We like to think that we're free, that we shape our own future, and that we need to protect our autonomy.

We are free, but the freedom we have comes from God. Our freedom has a purpose, and decision making is essentially a matter of discovering this purpose and aligning ourselves with it. God is at work in your life and cares about the decisions we make that shape our path.

The man who expressed this truth in a way that is especially convincing to us is Ignatius of Loyola, a Basque priest who lived and worked in Europe five hundred years ago. You will hear much about Ignatius in this book. He invented the methodology for decision making that we present here, and his insights into the spiritual dimension of discernment and the psychology of choosing have stood the test of time. Ignatius's book *The Spiritual Exercises* is one of the most insightful and influential books about spirituality ever written. At the beginning of the book, Ignatius laid out his presuppositions about God and human beings in a note called "Principle and Foundation." Here is part of it as translated by David L. Fleming, SJ, in a modern paraphrase. Wendy and everyone else facing a decision should begin here:

> God who loves us creates us and wants to share
> life with us forever. Our love response takes shape

in our praise and honor and service of the God of our life.

All the things in this world are also created because of God's love and they become a context of gifts, presented to us so that we can know God more easily and make a return of love more readily.

At the center of reality is a God who loves us, says Ignatius. The world God created is good. "All the things in this world" exist so that we can love better. Our decisions are choices about how we use the things in this world. Our decisions *matter* to God.

God cares. That's our first premise. Our second premise is that "God's will" is something more than a pious religious phrase.

WE CAN KNOW GOD'S WILL

Charlotte retired at age fifty-five, when she and her husband, Phil—and their financial planner—decided that they didn't need her income to build their retirement savings. She was glad to shut down her business as a freelance designer of educational software. She had enjoyed the work for many years, but the stress took a toll on her as she got older. She liked working with clients; she disliked the tedium of writing the software and the pressure of finding a steady stream of work. In retirement, Charlotte did some things she'd always wanted to do. She spent more time with her five grandchildren nearby. She volunteered at a nursing home and hospice. She took a painting class and worked on a committee to plan the annual art fair in her city. Sometimes she missed the challenge and satisfaction of her former work. Sometimes she felt restless. But she was happy.

One day, a former colleague called. His educational company had just landed a contract to develop software for a remedial reading program in the public schools. He offered Charlotte her dream job: she would head a group that defined the educational objectives of the program. And she would be working with reading teachers, which was the kind of work she loved. A bonus—she wouldn't have to write any code. The pay was excellent and the hours flexible. Her friend emphasized how much good Charlotte could do working on a successful program to help children read. Charlotte immediately said yes. "I felt like God himself was giving me this job," she said.

The kind of decisions we'll be talking about in this book are similar to Charlotte's—choices between two or more attractive, morally permissible alternatives. Charlotte could continue in a satisfying, productive retirement, or she could return to satisfying, productive work. This is not a choice between good and evil. There's no clear right or wrong option. The question for Charlotte—and for us, most of the time—is, Which is the better choice? If God cares, what is God's will?

"God's will" is a loaded, imprecise, and controversial phrase. The first problem is, What is the *nature* of God's will? One view is that God's will is completely objective, a plan made for us before we were born that exists independently of our desires, feelings, history, choices, and relationships. At the other extreme is the view that God's will is subjective; whatever we do to fulfill our potential and attain happiness is God's will.

The second problem has to do with *knowing* God's will. We sometimes run across people who are certain that they know what God's will is in specific matters: television preachers, religious zealots. They make us nervous—or envious. *Lucky you, to know what God's will is. I wish I did.* At the other extreme are people who don't have the slightest idea what God might want of them when they face an important decision, and so they think it's a waste of time even to ask. Their God is detached or indifferent or inaccessible.

Finally there's the problem of *doing* God's will. Some people think that, once they know what God wants, they can do it. It's simply a matter of willpower, of bold, decisive action. The view at the other extreme is that gravely flawed, easily tempted sinners like us are seldom able to do what God wants. We're bound to fail. (Interestingly, people at both extremes tend to think that God generally wants people to make heroic, difficult, and unpleasant gestures of renunciation.)

Ignatian discernment lies somewhere in the middle of all of these views. God's will is neither totally objective nor entirely subjective. It's a blend of both—God's desire for us manifests to a large degree in our own desires and struggles. God's will is something we can know, but we can't be sure that we know it perfectly. We are sinners with flawed minds and wayward hearts and an impressive capacity for self-delusion. In fact, the mechanics of Ignatian discernment consist largely of techniques to free ourselves of attachments to desires and ideas that lead us astray. Finally, Ignatian discernment holds that we're entirely capable of doing God's will once we properly discern it. But this is not a matter of simple willpower. Doing God's will is more a matter of grow-ing into the kind of person we're meant to be.

So, when Charlotte was offered her dream job out of the blue, she wasn't mistaken to think that God had something to say about the decision she faced. But her decision-making process? That's another matter.

OUR FEELINGS ARE A KEY TO DISCERNMENT

At age thirty, after much discussion and prayer, Anne decided to quit her job and go to graduate school. Many experienced people thought she had impres-sive literary talent. Her short stories had been praised. A couple of well-known fiction editors in New York were impressed by a draft of her novel. Anne wanted to learn her craft and see how far she could go as a writer. Her husband agreed with her decision. So they packed up and moved to the University of Iowa, where Anne started work on an MFA.

The decision stunned most of Anne's friends and family. She was a highly successful journalist in Los Angeles. She had won awards for her magazine writing, and at age twenty-eight she had become editor of a city magazine and boosted its circulation by 40 percent in two years. Most of Anne's friends thought she should pursue a journalism career in Los Angeles. Even some of her literary mentors thought she should keep her day job and write on the side. But Anne was firm in her decision to go to school.

Her first months in Iowa City were very difficult. Some aspects of the program disappointed her.

> *She didn't connect well with a couple of her teach-*
> *ers, and she didn't make any friends. Truth be told,*
> *Anne could barely write. Emotionally, she was up*
> *and down. When she was feeling low, plagued by*
> *thoughts that she had made a big mistake in choos-*
> *ing graduate school, she longed to go back to jour-*
> *nalism in California. At other times, she felt she had*
> *made the right decision. But sadness persisted, and*
> *she couldn't shake the idea of quitting and returning*
> *home. She began to seriously consider the idea.*

Anne doesn't know what to do. Her feelings pull her in one direction and then in the other. They seem to be a problem, but actually they are part of the solution. Her emotions contain valuable information about the direction life should take. Learning to interpret emotions is one of the best ways to discern God's will for our choices in life.

This was the key insight that our hero, Ignatius, had about the problem of decision making. When he faced an impor-tant decision, Ignatius would contemplate the alternatives and pay attention to how he felt about them. These feelings, he realized, often pointed the way to the best choice. Over the years, Ignatius became expert in interpreting these feel-ings. From him, we learn that the answers to the question, What is God asking of me? can be found in the inner move-ments of feelings within our hearts.

Five hundred years ago, many people thought this idea was dangerous nonsense. It remains a controversial idea in some circles today. Ignatius's view that our emotions can be trusted rests on an expansive, optimistic view of the relation-ship between God and human beings. Ignatius believed that God deals *directly* with us. God works in our minds; he also works in our feelings. Ignatius said that we can look at our human experience of life with a basic attitude of trust. This includes our desires and inclinations, our likes and dislikes, our highs and lows.

The contrary view—that our emotions are deceptive and troublesome—has a long and distinguished history. Thinkers from the ancient Greeks to Sigmund Freud have held that human emotions are a shifting sea of passion and illusion that we are well advised to master or ignore. The theological version of this outlook holds that natural human inclinations are misguided because of sin. They lead us, not toward, but away from God. We're to be suspicious of our feelings. Certainly we can't expect to find God speaking through them.

Echoes of this attitude resonate today. We value our emotions and prize them as the locus of the authentic self, but many of us are reluctant to make them an important part of decision making. The predominant cultural view is that reason and analysis are sounder bases for action than our feelings. The head trumps the heart. "That's just the way I feel," we say. Or worse, "I can't trust my own judgment."

You can trust your judgment and your feelings, Ignatius would say, and we agree. Anne's alternating moods of despair and satisfaction as she struggles in graduate school are full of spiritual meaning. The trick is to understand that meaning.

Ignatius can help us with this. He discovered some very practical ways of discerning, or sorting through, our emotions. His discoveries proved so useful that the process of decision making he developed is popularly referred to as discernment—that's the term we will use in this book. We will define discernment more clearly in chapter 4, but for now, we simply use the word to refer to the process of decision making.

There's a Methodology to Making Decisions

Charlie is the administrator of a large cardiovascular surgical unit at a university hospital. It's a demanding job; he routinely works fifty-hour weeks, sometimes more. A year ago, when the youngest of his three children started college, Charlie was freed up to take on some outside volunteer projects. He joined the board of a nonprofit organization that supports music education in the city's public elementary schools, with a particular focus on minorities and children of immigrants. Charlie has accomplished a great deal, raising substantial funding and helping recruit local musicians to volunteer their time. The program has been expanding. Charlie is very satisfied with his work. He loves music, and he likes the idea of helping young people learn to love it, too.

A month ago, two close friends of Charlie's asked him to join them on the board of a nonprofit organization that sponsors literacy education projects in the community. The group needs fund-raising help, some new ideas, a jolt of energy. Charlie is well equipped for all of this, and immediately he's drawn to the idea. He thinks about it for a while, and the answer seems clear: he says no to his friends. He doesn't have the time to serve on both boards, and his work in music education has been very productive. However, the idea of literacy education won't go away. Charlie keeps thinking about the invitation. He puts it aside; it keeps coming back. He wonders, Should I reconsider? Should I do this?

Who hasn't faced Charlie's dilemma? Two attractive options present themselves—job offers, career paths, volunteer opportunities, dates for Saturday night. You can't have both. The head says one thing and the heart says another. How do you sort it out?

Ignatius's first great contribution to the discussion was his realization that our emotions are an important factor in decision making. His second achievement—even more important, in our view—was to develop a methodology for decision making that can be usefully applied to situations like Charlie's. Our feelings have to be interpreted; we shouldn't always just go with our gut, at least in most situations. And feelings aren't the only consideration. Analysis is part of decision making, too, as are our life circumstances, the advice of others, and prior commitments and decisions. Most of this book elaborates on the method Ignatius developed to make sense of all these factors.

It took Ignatius many years to develop his method. Some of his initial stabs at discernment were primitive. Shortly after his conversion, he was traveling down a road in rural Spain in the company of an argumentative Muslim. The Muslim said something insulting about the Blessed Virgin Mary and galloped away. Ignatius's first impulse was to go after the Muslim to avenge the insult. His second impulse was to let it go. The conflicted Ignatius let his donkey make the decision. He would kill the Muslim if the donkey took one fork in the road. He would ride away peacefully if the beast took the other road. The donkey took the peaceful route.

Ignatius soon acquired enough maturity as a Christian to be able to make such decisions without the help of his donkey. But a couple of important points were clear even at this very early stage. He knew what it meant to be torn between two impulses. He had the good sense to hesitate—to reflect before making a decision. And he understood that he needed help when the decision wasn't clear. The story reveals another facet of Ignatius's personality. He told the story himself in his *Autobiography* many years later, when he was an esteemed churchman and the head of a dynamic new religious order. He didn't mind telling a story that made him look a little foolish; it seems that he took pains to show that not even the great Ignatius had all the answers.

But Ignatius had enough answers to the problem of decision making that millions of people throughout the centuries have looked to him for guidance. He developed a method and an approach. His advice about interpreting the inner movements of the heart is summarized in "Rules for Discernment of Spirits." He proposed three methods for making decisions and fleshed out how these methods work in practical terms. Ignatian decision making works best when we can listen and reflect on our experience and develop sensitivity to subtle spiritual signals. Ignatius gave us tools to help us acquire these skills as well.

People like Charlie can dig into an Ignatian tool kit to make their way forward when the road seems unclear.

DECISIONS LEAD
TO MORE DECISIONS

Jon was bored at his job as an information technology engineer for a real estate company. He wanted to do something that served people's needs more directly. His friends encouraged him to make a change, as did his pastor and a couple of other people whom he thought had spiritual insight. He considered several options: going to graduate school for a degree in social work; living off his savings for a year while he did volunteer work, took some courses, and considered his future; or joining a friend in a new company that helped nonprofit agencies with their fund-raising and business operations.

Jon did none of these things. He decided to travel and taste some adventure while he was still young and single, so he went to Uganda to help a small nongovernmental organization set up and operate AIDS clinics. It was a disastrous experience. The job was enormously stressful. He was unprepared for African culture. He was disheartened by Ugandan poverty and the vast scope of the AIDS crisis. He fell ill with an intestinal ailment that didn't go away. Six months into the job—lonely, sick, and depressed—he quit and came home. He wanted to find out what went wrong and what he should do next.

Uganda seemed like a good idea at the time, but it was pretty clearly the wrong place for Jon. Now, Jon has more decisions to make. Part of the process is to look back on his African adventure and learn from it. He'll also evaluate the thinking that led to the decision to go there. He'll look at why he was bored at his former job. And he'll take a closer look at what he really wants from life.

The point is that decisions lead to more decisions. It can be narrow and misleading to think of decision making in terms of a single decision. The model is a journey. The end is "life forever with God," in the words of Ignatius's "Principle and Foundation." The road to this end is a meandering one. Our travels are punctuated by decisions, some of them crucial, even life changing, but we seldom arrive at a point where no further decisions are necessary.

Ignatian decision making isn't linear. It's more of a spiraling circle. We reflect on our experience, make a decision based on reflection and discernment, put the decision into practice, experience the result, reflect on that experience, and so forth. It's a circular process that carries us deeper and forward into a life lived with God.

Thus, even our mistakes can be useful material in the next decision. In fact, it's hard to think of a decision that is absolutely bad with no redeeming qualities and possibilities. As long as we're walking the road with open-mindedness, as long as we're seeking to do good and to love God and our fellow human beings, we'll continue to grow and learn. Jon probably shouldn't have gone to Uganda. Anne might have made a mistake in going to graduate school. You might be badly overcommitted because of your unfortunate tendency to agree to do more work without thinking about it. But you can do better next time—in part because you can learn from what didn't go especially well.

We don't have to have it all together to make sound decisions. We don't have to be perfect. We don't need to be deterred by imperfect knowledge and murky circumstances. If we are earnestly seeking God, we won't go far wrong.

The fact is this: *the decision is not the goal.* That may sound like a Zen paradox, but it's actually quite consistent with our premises. The goal is to grow in a relationship with God. The decisions we make are means to this end. Ignatius put it this way in his "Principle and Foundation" at the beginning of the *Spiritual Exercises*: "Our one choice should be this: I want and I choose what better leads to God's deepening life in me."

The only prerequisite for good decision making is a desire to make this one choice to grow in life with God. This is a demanding requirement, as you will see. But it's not a requirement that involves a lot of religious doctrine or specific religious practices. A desire to grow in a relationship with God means that we believe that God is a personal being who loves us, who is active in the world and in our lives, and whose mind is accessible to us through prayer and discernment. These are broadly Christian beliefs. We are Christians, and Ignatius developed his approach to discernment in a Christian context. But the beliefs that are key to discernment are not creeds and dogmas. The necessary spiritual practices involve personal prayer and reflection.

That's not to say that doctrines and churchgoing are unimportant. They are, and they can be tremendously helpful in living out whatever decisions you come to. But that's a discussion for another day. What you need to go forward with Ignatian discernment is a sincere desire to choose the good and a conviction that God cares about you.

Armed with these ideas, you're ready to tackle the first big question: Why are decisions so tough?

CHAPTER 2

Why Are Good Decisions So Hard to Make?

In July 2008, the Sunday *New York Times* told the sad story of Diane McLeod, a fortyish Philadelphia woman whom the *Times* presented as a poster child of the nation's bad debt-fueled economic crisis. McLeod's finances were in shambles. For years she had spent more money than she made. She would buy whatever she wanted on credit, and when her credit card debt became too high, she would pay it off by refinancing her house. Her financial ship sank when she lost her job and home values fell. The mortgage company foreclosed on her home, and McLeod filed for bankruptcy.

Who's to blame for this? the *Times* asked. McLeod or the finance companies that kept lending money to a woman with a low income and a bad credit rating? Both, of course. McLeod took responsibility for her actions. She admitted that it was a bad idea to do things like go on a shopping spree to make herself feel better after her marriage broke up and spend hours shopping on the QVC television channel while she was recovering from surgery. But McLeod had plenty of help. Banks and credit card companies eagerly extended credit to her even as she missed monthly payments and her credit rating sank.

The *New York Times* told McLeod's story because it illuminates some of the reasons for America's economic woes. It interests us because of the light it casts on decision making. McLeod made bad financial decisions, but they didn't seem to be choices made as the result of a conscious, rational process. She absorbed powerful cultural messages such as "Get what you want now" and "Don't be afraid of debt." Our society tells us that it's okay to shop, spend, and travel freely: "There are some things that money can't buy. For everything else there's MasterCard."

The advertising executive behind MasterCard's Priceless campaign explained the problem his client needed to solve: "One of the tricks in the credit card business is that people have an inherent guilt with spending," said Jonathan B. Cranin, of the McCann Erickson advertising agency. "What you want is to have people feel good about their purchases."

What we want is the freedom necessary to make good choices. Standing in the way of this freedom are many of the cultural norms and values that we grow up with and unconsciously adopt as our own. Our culture's attitude toward spending and debt is a good example. Not too long ago our culture frowned on debt. Paying our own way was virtuous; going into debt was a vice. Today, we Americans live in a world where the ability to borrow is a virtue and being forced to pay as you go is a misfortune, or at least is perceived as backward. The availability of easy credit is a blessing in many ways. We need mortgages to buy homes and student loans to get an education. But it can also be a temptation and a trap, as Diane McLeod and millions of other Americans have learned.

Our choices take place within a certain culture that has definite ideas about what we should value, what we should ignore, and what we should strive for. We need to understand those values to make good decisions. We don't necessarily have to reject these cultural values, but we must not let them carry us away as though we were sticks on a fast-flowing river. Ignatius recommended that we "hold ourselves in balance before all created gifts." To do this, we must first coolly appraise what our culture says is important.

WALT WHITMAN AND THE RISE OF EXPRESSIVE INDIVIDUALISM

Perhaps the paramount value of American culture is individualism, the outlook that stresses independence, self-reliance, and individual liberty. These values are enshrined in the founding documents of the United States, and the nation has since been populated by many people seeking freedom from oppressive rulers, religious authorities, and more traditional social systems. Individualists dislike the idea that societal, group, or national goals should take priority over an individual's goals. In general, individualists are suspicious of tradition, religion, or any other form of external moral standard that is used to limit an individual's choices. When it comes to making decisions, individualists want no outside interference.

Thus, to pursue our personal goals, we move to new cities, change careers, start new ventures, take up new hobbies, and drop old relationships. There's great energy and creativity in all this activity, but there's a downside, too. Our individualism tends to isolate us. It weakens ties to family and community. Not many people have in our homes what the social scientists Will Miller and Glenn Sparks call "refrigerator rights"—relationships with friends that are so warm and trusting that friends can come over and help themselves to a casual snack.

Instead, we have "parasocial" relationships, or so-called relationships with celebrities, athletic teams, reality-television stars, and purely fictional characters on soap operas and serial television dramas. They aren't really relationships because they are entirely one sided. You can watch Oprah Winfrey every day and learn all about her life, but she knows nothing about you. Social scientists have noted the rise of weak relationships—Facebook friends, Twitter buddies, and online video-game partners. These relationships are weak because the parties involved control what they reveal of themselves. You can even fashion a wholly new identity. Think of that great *New Yorker* cartoon with two dogs, where one says to the other, "On the Internet, no one has to know you're a dog."

Classical individualism celebrated political and economic freedom. But modern individualism has added an expressive quality. The individual is considered the center of the moral universe. This expressive individualism is the spirit of Walt Whitman's famous epic poem immodestly titled "Song of Myself," which begins:

> I celebrate myself, and sing myself,
> And what I assume you shall assume,
> For every atom belonging to me as good belongs
>   to you.

Expressive individualism proclaims, as Whitman put it, "Nor do I understand who there can be more wonderful than myself." In this worldview, the goal of our lives is to fulfill ourselves. The means to this end are the choices we make. The social scientist Robert Bellah describes the moral shift that is expressive individualism this way: "Its genius is that it enables the individual to think of commitments—from marriage and work to political and religious involvement—as enhancements of the sense of individual well-being rather than moral imperatives." This attitude is epitomized in the ballad made famous by Frank Sinatra, "I Did It My Way."

This shift is subtle. Individual well-being is not unimportant; we do need to consider it in decision making. But when our personal fulfilment becomes the paramount consideration, we are adrift in a sea of relativism. External moral propositions and ethical claims give way to an individual's personal judgment about what is meaningful and what isn't. In moral relativism, there are no absolute rights and wrongs, only different situations.

Because of this moral relativism, a spirit of utilitarian efficiency animates our individualistic culture. Without external moral norms, the end justifies the means. If the end is personal fulfillment (however we define it), the best choice is the one that gets us to that end quickly and efficiently. We measure ourselves by what we are able to accomplish, and we judge others by how well they function. In other words, we're after results. The utilitarian spirit thinks very little of the advice of the poet Rainer Maria Rilke in his "Letters to a Young Poet":

> Be patient toward all that is unsolved in your heart and try to love the questions themselves like locked rooms and like books that are written in a very foreign tongue. Do not now seek the answers, which cannot be given you because you

> would not be able to live them. And the point
> is, to live everything. Live the questions now.
> Perhaps you will then gradually, without noticing
> it, live along some distant day into the answer.

It's important not to characterize the current cultural values as bad; they are points of view that contain wisdom as well as pitfalls. Individual liberty is an important human right, and our personal well-being is a proper consideration when we make decisions. A desire to accomplish things efficiently is admirable. And we don't want to simply conform ourselves to someone else's notion of what we should do.

But the pitfalls are real, and they are all the more hazardous because their influence is hidden. The truth is that the current cultural values aren't the only values, and they are not as central to good decision making as our culture says they are. It is very difficult to stand apart from our culture and its ideas of what's important and what's not.

Consider Wendy, the medical student we met in the first chapter who is trying to decide whether to marry Robert, the ambitious MBA student. Wendy is relatively indifferent to the lure of wealth and status that motivates Robert, but she cannot ignore money. Nor can she be so sure that her desire to help drug addicts in a significant way is an entirely selfless goal. It may involve a desire to achieve personal fulfillment and the acclaim of others in a different way. We need to examine our motives carefully and take a hard look at what we think constitutes a good life.

Here's an experiment to illustrate the subtlety of the value problem. Say that you are recruiting volunteers for a program that helps recent immigrants learn English. What would you say to get people to sign up? You would probably say, "Oh, you're going to love it." "You'll have fun." "The people you help will love you for it." "The work isn't too hard." "You'll feel good about yourself." "The hours are flexible—it's easy to fit it into your schedule." This sales pitch isn't completely true. This kind of work isn't exactly fun; in fact, it can be tedious and difficult. The clients aren't always openly grateful. And it is always hard to honor a volunteer commitment week after week. Nevertheless, you say things like this because you assume that people want to do volunteer work to make themselves happy.

You are not wrong to make this assumption. In John's Gospel (15:11), Jesus says, "I have told you this so that my joy may be in you and your joy might be complete." But the joy that Jesus is talking about is something deeper and more solid than a transitory feeling of contentment at having helped someone less fortunate than you are. The goal of discernment isn't to have positive feelings about oneself. Our purpose in life, as Ignatius expressed it, is "to praise, reverence, and serve God our Lord." This includes personal happiness, because our joy must be complete, but it is a deeper happiness than that which is commonly thought of in our culture.

A BIGGER PROBLEM

Troublesome cultural messages complicate decision making, but the culture problem is only a symptom of a bigger problem: our divided hearts. We want contradictory things. We want it all. Our hearts impatiently lurch from one choice to another as conflicting desires wax and wane. This is a spiritual problem.

That problem is built into the very nature of making choices. God's will is usually difficult to discern, and our awareness of

God's presence is often dim. We are free to choose, and this freedom is a curse as well as a blessing. Bad human choices cause most of the misery and suffering in the world—we can choose evil as well as good. We can be selfish or generous, cruel or kind, vengeful or forgiving. We can pursue personal glory, or we can work for the good of other people.

Why? Why did God give men and women the ability to reject the good? Why do we grope around in the dark, struggling with our decisions, wondering what to do? Why isn't God more present to us?

This is one of the oldest philosophical questions, a conundrum without a satisfactory solution, because we cannot read God's mind. But we can be sure of one thing: our freedom must be important to God—otherwise we wouldn't have it. C. S. Lewis put it well in his book *The Screwtape Letters*, a work of theological satire that features thirty-one letters written by a senior demon named Screwtape to his nephew, a young demon named Wormwood. Here Screwtape explains the ways of God (the Enemy):

> You must have wondered why the Enemy does not make more use of His power to be sensibly present to human souls in any degree He chooses and at any moment. But now you see that the Irresistible and the Indisputable are the two weapons which the very nature of His scheme forbids Him to use. Merely to over-ride a human will (as His felt presence in any but the faintest and most mitigated degree would certainly do) would be for Him useless. He cannot ravish. He can only woo. For His ignoble idea is to eat the cake and have it; the creatures are to be one with Him, but themselves. . . .

He wants them to learn to walk and must therefore take away His hand; and if only the will to walk is really there He is pleased even with their stumbles. Do not be deceived, Wormwood. Our cause is never more in danger than when a human, no longer desiring, but still intending to do our Enemy's will, looks round upon a universe from which every trace of Him seems to have vanished, and asks why he has been forsaken, and still obeys.

Our decisions matter, and we are truly free to make them.

A song by Michael John Poirier called "Hello, Lord" captures the essence of the problem. The song is a prayer about how difficult it is to pray. The singer's problem is a gravely divided heart:

> Part of me wants to follow
> Part of me wants to leave . . .
>
> Part of me wants to trust you.
> Part of me wants control . . .
>
> Part of me wants to know you.
> Part of me turns away.

A divided heart and perfect freedom—what a dilemma! A part of us genuinely desires to know God's will and to live a life of greater goodness and integrity. But a part of us resists that desire and is suspicious of any interaction with God. This part of us wants to take control. Our struggle between trust and suspicion, between faith and doubt, between surrender and control, takes place on a spiritual terrain where we have freedom to choose. The restless desire lurking in the background of decision making is the desire to have it all. It's hard to choose, because making a decision means saying no as much as it means saying yes, and we hate to say no to ourselves. That's why the traditional Christian marriage vows include a promise to forsake all others. This is the flip side of the partners' promise to love each other exclusively. Committing oneself to one partner means leaving all others behind. Every important decision involves roads not taken, possibilities forever unexplored, work that we will never do, people who will not be part of our lives. We often long for the alternative that we did not select and experience its absence as an actual loss.

Loss is painful. Behavioral studies show that most human beings feel a loss more keenly than a gain. Investors hate losing money more than they love making it. Loss aversion drives people to make unwise decisions, such as hanging on to a bad investment too long to avoid taking a loss, or cashing in good investments too soon for fear of losing any gains they had made. Because we fear loss, we make less-than-wholehearted decisions, hesitant decisions, circumscribed decisions, or no decisions at all—anything to avoid that pang of hindsight regret: I should have chosen that job, that partner, that school.

THE SOLUTION: DISCERNMENT

Decision making is a struggle, yet the Ignatian approach accepts the struggle wholeheartedly. In fact, the approach to decision making that Ignatius suggests *depends* on this struggle. It claims that the signs of God's direction for our lives are found precisely in the shifting movements of our divided hearts as spiritual forces struggle for mastery. Ignatian discernment teaches us to become aware of those movements, to reflect on them, and to interpret them. The battle is the problem, but it is also the solution.

The point has often been made that the Christian Gospel is a story of strength and triumph arising from weakness and defeat. The Savior is a poor man in a provincial, backwater land. Salvation comes about through suffering and death. In the words of Mary's Magnificat prayer: "He has brought down the powerful from their thrones, and lifted up the lowly; he has filled the hungry with good things, and sent the rich away empty."

We're afflicted with divided hearts that cause us to be burdened by angst, uncertainty, and fear when making important decisions. But this very confusion of thoughts and feelings is the place where we find God's footprints. It's the raw material for discernment.

This was Ignatius's great discovery.

CHAPTER 3

Ignatius of Loyola's Big Discovery

Ignatius of Loyola ranks as a major figure in both secular and religious history. He founded the Society of Jesus, better known as the Jesuits, which in his own lifetime became a worldwide missionary order, a major force in the sixteenth-century renewal of Catholicism, and creator of an educational system that transformed Europe and beyond. His spiritual ideas have had a lasting impact on the way people think about the relationship between God and human beings. Ignatian spirituality has given rise to generations of contemplatives-in-action—men and women who seek union with God by uniting themselves with God's work in the world. Ignatius's *Spiritual Exercises* is one of the most influential books on prayer and the spiritual life ever written.

Ignatius did not gain his insights into the spiritual life by deep study or sudden revelation from God. They were the fruits of years of patient observation and trial and error. He noticed how God dealt with him and with other men and women. He spent many years helping people grow closer to God. Ignatian spirituality is not a constructed spiritual system; it's a series of discoveries about the spiritual life that are rooted in pragmatic testing. Ignatius noticed what worked and what didn't. This makes his insights into decision making and his rules for discernment especially valuable. Ignatius didn't invent them, but he did discover them long before the development of modern psychology and its naming of our interior processes.

For the first half of his life, Ignatius gave no one any reason to think that he was destined to become one of history's most influential religious leaders. He was born in 1491, the youngest of thirteen children in a family of minor nobility in the region of Azpeitia in northern Spain. He was an ethnic Basque—tough, passionate, and strong willed. Ignatius demonstrated these qualities in abundance when, as a young man, he went to serve at the court of the Kingdom of Castile. There, in his own words, "he was man given over to the vanities of the world, and took a special delight in the exercise of arms, with a great and vain desire of winning glory." The young Ignatius was a street fighter. He was accused of meddling with another man's wife (or mistress). He dreamed of impressing women with his courage and feats of military prowess.

Ignatius got his chance to impress in 1521, when he led the Spanish defense of the city of Pamplona against a French attack. The defenders were badly outnumbered, but Ignatius rallied them for a while. But then a French cannonball came over the wall of the city and struck Ignatius in the legs. Both were broken, one of them quite badly with a compound fracture. With their leader incapacitated, the Spanish defenders surrendered the city. The chivalrous French, admiring Ignatius's courage and no doubt sure that his military career was over, allowed him to go home to his town of Loyola.

In Loyola he endured two excruciating operations to repair his damaged legs. He nearly died after the first operation, an experience that seems to have prompted the first stirrings of an active faith. But spiritual change came slowly to Ignatius. He ordered a second operation for cosmetic purposes, thinking that the leg's unsightly appearance would make it hard for him to cut a dashing figure when he returned to the royal court.

Facing many months of convalescence in his family's castle (actually a dark, nondescript silolike structure that still stands today), the restless, hyperactive Ignatius became intolerably bored. He asked his sister-in-law to bring him some romances to read. Thrillers and romances were the most popular reading materials in Ignatius's day, as they are in ours, and Ignatius loved to read such tales of dangerous quests, narrow escapes, and knightly adventures carried out to stir the hearts of noble maidens. Alas, the Loyola household contained no such books; instead, Ignatius was given a book on the life of Christ and a collection of stories about the saints. These topics held little interest for Ignatius, but he was so bored that he read the books anyway.

In reading about the saints, he became quite inspired. The story of St. Francis of Assisi paralleled his own life: as was Ignatius, Francis was a passionate young man from a comfortable background who was wounded in battle and captured. God used this misfortune to stir Francis's soul profoundly. *I could do that, too, even better than Francis did,* Ignatius thought. He felt the same way about St. Dominic. He was thrilled with the idea of going from place to place preaching the Gospel. This is how Ignatius began his conversion—with a sense of competition with the heroic saints of the past! It was like the song "I Can Do That," in the musical *A Chorus Line,* where someone does a dance step and the other person says, "I can do that, and I can even do it better."

After a while, the lure of the saints diminished, and Ignatius put his books aside and daydreamed about the joys of courtly life. He'd think about his lady loves and relish memories of successful battles. He'd proudly recall the righteous power he felt when entering battle in the name of God and the king. He'd remember how he had dealt with the people who had insulted him and how good it felt to defend his honor. When these memories grew stale, Ignatius returned to the lives of the saints and imagined how good it would be to live a life of prayer and contemplation. Then he would return to his daydreams of knightly valor. He'd go back-and-forth in his imaginative life—dreams of following Jesus alternated with dreams of romance.

He noticed that his emotions were unsettled. Some days he would feel happy and content; other days he would be restless and troubled. He began to keep track of his feelings and reflect on them. Eventually, the lightbulb went on: his feelings were related to his imaginative life. All of his daydreams pleased him while he was dreaming, but the emotional aftermath differed. He was calm and peaceful after he dreamed of following Christ. He was agitated and sad after daydreaming of machismo, lust, and honor.

Ignatius realized that these feelings had spiritual meaning. They weren't merely responses to the pain of enforced idleness—or what today we would attribute to brain chemistry or psychological coping strategies. God was communicating with him through his emotions. Without really intending to, Ignatius had stumbled upon one of the secrets of discernment. His fantasies were not simply daydreams; they represented two directions his life could take. God was using his feelings about these choices to point him in the direction that was best for him to go.

This insight was the beginning of Ignatius's conversion. It would eventually lead him to a great career as a spiritual director, churchman, and saint (something that unfolded slowly). Ignatius saw that God was speaking to him. He was filled with a sincere desire to love and serve God—the one prerequisite for good discernment. This insight also was the beginning of his understanding of discernment principles. Ignatius saw important distinctions between his different feelings. There was a big difference between the gnawing anxiety he would feel sometimes and the inspiration and tranquility he experienced other times. He also noticed times of spiritual "consolations" that involved some positive feelings. He contrasted that with spiritual desolation, which involved opposite feelings, such as turmoil within.

Ignatius's great discovery was that we can listen to the language of our hearts when making decisions. Many factors help in this process: following general principles, asking for the advice of friends and mentors, analyzing the pros and cons of alternative courses of action. To these, Ignatius added finding the spiritual meaning of our emotions. Ignatius recognized that we could trust our experience. This was an insight into the way God puts human beings together. We're designed to hear God speak through our emotional responses to the experiences we have.

THE GOD OF IGNATIUS AND THE GOD OF HUCKLEBERRY FINN

We risk getting ahead of ourselves. Ignatius's insights into discernment rest on a certain understanding about what God is like. As he lay in the Loyola castle recovering from his wounds, Ignatius came to understand that God is not an exacting judge, a wizard pulling the strings behind the curtain, or a remote divinity far removed from human affairs. Rather, he experienced a God who loves, a God who is actively involved in our affairs and who invites us to respond to love by loving in return.

Learning that God can be understood in this way is an important insight, crucial to decision making. What kind of a world do we live in? Do we believe that God exists? If we do, can we trust God as the one who presides over all things? Do we approach decision making by thinking that we have to measure up to a rigorous standard? Do we feel alone? Or do we have a sense that God is with us? Our answers to these questions deeply influence the way we make our choices.

Our image of God matters. Consider the difference between the God of Ignatius and the God of Huckleberry Finn.

One of the dramatic high points in Mark Twain's great novel *Adventures of Huckleberry Finn* occurs when Huck Finn struggles with his conscience over what to do about his friend and companion on the river, the escaped slave Jim. Huck has been raised by whites in the South who use the Bible and Christianity to justify and defend slavery. Jim is a slave who belongs to Miss Watson. Huck believes that it was wrong for Jim to escape, and that it is gravely sinful for a white person like himself to help Jim run away. His Christian duty is to turn Jim in. But Jim is Huck's friend and companion, and Huck doesn't want to return him to slavery. At the same time, Huck is terrified by God—or, rather, by the image of God that has been instilled in him:

> It hit me all of a sudden that here was the plain hand of Providence slapping me in the face and letting me know my wickedness was being watched all the time from up there in heaven, whilst I was stealing a poor old woman's negro that hadn't ever done me no harm, and now was showing me there's One that's always on the

lookout, and ain't agoing to allow no such miserable doings to go only just so fur and no further, I
most dropped in my tracks I was so scared.

Huck's idea of God torments him. Eventually, he does the
right thing; he rejects the idea of returning Jim to his master—"All right, then, I'll go to hell," he declares. Mark Twain
portrays this as a great act of moral courage, and indeed it is,
but only because Huck is burdened by a mistaken image of
God. Ironically, Huck's mental image of Jim bears many of
the divine qualities in Ignatius's understanding of God:

I'd see him standing my watch on top of his'n,
stead of calling me, so I could go on sleeping; and
see him how glad he was when I come back out
of the fog; and when I come to him again in the
swamp up there where the feud was; and such-like
times, and would always call me honey, and pet
me, and do everthing he could think of for me,
and how good he always was.

Huck's struggle is a battle between two images—the image of
a strict, censorious God and the image of the gentle, trustworthy Jim.

Ignatius's image of God was very different from Huck
Finn's. "God who loves us creates us and wants to share
his life with us forever," he writes in his "Principle and
Foundation" at the beginning of the *Spiritual Exercises* (in
a modern paraphrase). Later in the Exercises, he asks us to
imagine God—conceived as a Trinity of Father, Son, and Holy
Spirit—looking on the world in all its splendor and suffering:
"the happy and the sad, so many people aimless, despairing,
hateful, and killing, so many undernourished, sick and dying,

so many struggling with life and blind to any meaning. With God I can hear people laughing and cursing, some shouting and screaming, some praying, others cursing." God's answer to this spectacle is to say, "Let us work for the redemption of the whole human race." The remedy is Jesus. God enters into our suffering by sharing it. Jesus comes to heal and redeem. Jesus "does all this for me," Ignatius writes.

Ignatius does not claim that we can know everything about God. The totality of God is beyond our knowing. What we have are images of God—pictures in our minds that capture part of God's essence. These images are powerful, and they influence us in many ways as we make choices.

Take Steve, for example, a young man who came to us for counsel. Steve was struggling with a persistent sense of guilt. He had been raised a Catholic but for many years had "fallen away from the Church," as he put it. Meanwhile, he lived a life of service to others, spending several years in the Jesuit Volunteer Corps, a service organization, and then working in a homeless shelter. He had resumed his practice of a Catholic life largely through the influence of devout Catholics whom he worked with at the shelter. Nevertheless, Steve felt guilty. He felt terrible about his years away from Mass, and he thought he would never measure up to the standards expected of a "good" Catholic.

It helped Steve to ask himself, "What do I think God is like?" Steve thought that God was essentially a vengeful judge with an arbitrary streak. This God was interested in externals—rituals, accomplishments, things done and undone—that had little relation to Steve's internal life. But he came to see this as a distorted image of God. He began to see that he had been following God all his life; his personal experience was full of encounters with God. So gradually, he replaced his image of the harsh, score-keeping God with the image of a loving God who was constantly presenting him with opportunities to return that love.

Steve's judge–police officer god is only one of the distorted images that can plant themselves in our minds. There's the vengeful god who is out to punish us for the wrong we have done. There's the arbitrary god who is unpredictable and remote. There's the magical Santa Claus god who gives us whatever we want as long as we ask for it in the right way. There's the mafioso godfather god who will treat us well if we court his favor.

The point of all this is not to be critical of people whose image of God is distorted in some way or even to labor to come up with a "correct" image of God for ourselves. *The point is to notice how our ideas of God help or hinder our discernment.* Our images of God are not always helpful. They can get us off track. They can make it harder for us to freely choose the good when we are making decisions.

Ignatius taught us to set out on the journey of discernment grounded in this image of a generous, loving God. He continually returned to one aspect of God's character: our God *shares* with us. "Consider how God labors and works for us," he writes. He constantly advised those who were discerning their course in life to reflect on God's creative work, infinite blessings, and astounding generosity and to think, *God did all this for me.*

TRUST, SIMPLICITY, AND OTHER LESSONS LEARNED ON THE JOURNEY

Earlier we implied that Ignatius's insight into God's character preceded his big discovery about the importance of feelings in discernment. But that is not quite right. His understanding of

God unfolded gradually. Everything that Ignatius discovered took time. He put together his methodology for discernment through trial and error. His own life story puts to rest the myth that saints are superhuman and have it all together from the beginning.

Ignatius's first decision once he was able to travel was to go to Jerusalem and spend his life converting Muslims in the Holy Land. This is what serious Christians in his social class were supposed to do. On his way, he stopped at a village in Spain called Manresa for what he intended to be a short visit. He stayed there for a year—and it was a harrowing year at that. He experienced a real distaste for anything that had to do with God; there were persistent waves of discouragement about the way of life he was taking up; serious illnesses brought him again to the point of death; he became so obsessed with scruples that he became suicidal; he experienced consolations so powerful that they made his eyes hurt with weeping. These experiences taught him how to distinguish among true and false forms of encouragement, enthusiasm, and other pleasant and satisfying feelings.

Eventually, he reached Jerusalem but then discovered that he couldn't stay. The Franciscans, who oversaw the Christian holy places, were afraid that he would be kidnapped and held for ransom, so they told him he had to leave. Ignatius had to discern the purpose of his life all over again. He decided that God wanted him to teach the faith. To do that, he would have to get an education. He received his degree only after years of study at three universities. Several times his spiritual insights absorbed so much of his attention that his studies suffered. The Inquisition, suspicious of his spiritual ideas, put him in prison twice and put him on trial once (he was acquitted of heresy charges). He wanted to form a group of companions, but his first group broke up, causing him to be discouraged. Later, Ignatius did find a group of men who became the nucleus of the Society of Jesus, but it took a long time for the Society to settle on its mission. Many church authorities opposed a new order that did not pray the liturgy of the hours in a monastery but rather worked actively in the world.

Near the end of his life, Ignatius described this meandering journey in an autobiography. He referred to himself in the third person as "the pilgrim." He wrote that, all that time, God had been dealing with him in the same way that a schoolmaster deals with a child while instructing him or her. It was a course of education, of learning, but it was learning of a particular sort. The wisdom Ignatius acquired and the methodology he developed were founded on his personal experience. He learned a great deal from teachers and books, but these amplified and refined the lessons he learned through prayer, observation, and engagement with other people.

The story of Ignatius illustrates four truths that are crucial for the process of making decisions.

1. We can trust our experience.

Knowing that we can trust our experience is the first, and perhaps the most fundamental, lesson about discernment. Books and ideas and the counsel of the wise are all well and good, but the main arena for discernment is what we ourselves experience. We can discern the right direction by thoughtful reflection on our relationships with others, on our work in the world, and on the feelings those encounters generate. They are meaningful because God is in them. Our life is the classroom in which the Schoolmaster teaches and guides us.

Whole systems of thought and belief challenge this idea. Ancient philosophical traditions held that the physical world of matter and human bodies was a corrupt reflection of ideal forms that existed in the heavens. A theological tradition that began with Augustine and blossomed in Calvinism holds that sin hopelessly corrupts human judgment and reason, and that emotions are particularly suspect. One of the key ideas of Eastern religions is that this world is essentially an illusion and that enlightenment comes as we rid ourselves of desires and ambitions and feelings.

In this argument, Ignatius stands firmly on the side of human experience. It is real; it is meaningful; it is trustworthy when we understand it properly.

2. God deals with us directly.

We can trust our experience because God deals with us directly. Ignatius certainly believed that the church and Scripture are trustworthy teachers of truth and that we need that truth to help us interpret our experience. He also believed that Christians receive spiritual nourishment in the sacraments and in devotional prayer. But he also believed that God communicates directly to each of us. We can have a personal relationship with God. Prayer in the Ignatian mode is essentially a conversation. He warned spiritual directors not to get in the way. "Leave the creator to act immediately with the creature," he wrote.

3. Value the journey itself.

When we are facing a decision, we're usually anxious to be done with it: "Make up your mind and move on." We don't like the period of uncertainty, of hemming and hawing, of mulling things over, that precedes the decision. But for Ignatius, the run-up to the decision is the crucial time. This is the time of discernment, of prayer and reflection, of listening for the still, small voice of God. And the decision itself, however important it may be, is but one step in the journey of our lives. Pilgrimages are journeys to a holy place. The tradition of religious pilgrimages holds that the journey is at least as important as the goal. That is where the spiritual benefits lie.

4. We don't have to have it all together to make good decisions.

It's okay to have made mistakes, to struggle with persistent problems, to fall short of an ideal of mastery. The goal is not perfection but progress in relationship with God.

Ignatius's life illustrates these truths—especially the last two. God spoke to him directly and guided him on a pilgrimage. As he made his pilgrim journey, he learned to distinguish between deeply true notions of his destiny and those that were more superficial and even false. Thus, he came to know himself better. He did this by trial and error and even made mistakes along the way. He made decisions that seemed to take him down blind alleys. He had to retrace his steps, regroup, and figure things out all over again. In all these wanderings, he noticed that the true God did not castigate him for errors but lovingly helped him learn from them. This helped him to trust God more and to be more open. His pilgrimage was one of an ever-deepening and ever-strengthening relationship between his true self and the loving God he was coming to know. So it was that he was able to say in the *Spiritual Exercises* that we should pray for the grace to know God more intimately, which will allow us to love God more truly and follow him more closely.

That is why we look to this man who lived five hundred years ago for guidance and inspiration. Ignatius learned how to translate his powerful desires into practical decisions that shaped his life. He learned how to grow in day-by-day responsiveness to God. He learned discernment. This was Ignatius's big discovery, a breakthrough that changed the way we think about decisions.

CHAPTER 4

The One Thing Necessary (And a Few Other Things That Are Very Helpful)

Decisions are hard because they seem to be so complex. We frequently meet people who are paralyzed by the choices before them. They ponder an abundance of possible careers and courses of study, a surplus of potential relationships, a confusing mixture of pros and cons and conflicting advice. Some of this complexity is self-inflicted, but much of it is real. Our divided hearts stagger and stumble before the near-infinite menu of choices that modern life offers us. Where to begin? What is important, and what is extraneous?

LOVE GOD FIRST

One of Ignatius's greatest contributions to our understanding of decision making—perhaps the greatest contribution—is to simplify it radically. He thought that only one thing is truly necessary to make a good decision. If we get that one thing right, everything else will fall into place. If we get it wrong, or if we apply it haphazardly, trouble awaits us. This one necessary thing focuses our attention and clarifies what decision making is all about. It simplifies the challenge, but it doesn't necessarily make it easier.

The one necessary thing is this: *love God first.* Understand that you are in a relationship with God, who loves you and who desires the best for you. Approach your decisions as ways to cultivate and deepen this relationship. In the *Spiritual Exercises*, Ignatius said that we should approach our decisions "only looking for what we are created for." He said, "I ought to do whatever I do, that it may help me for the end for which I am created, not ordering or bringing the end to the means, but the means to the end."

Let's unpack this idea. Ignatius says, first, that we need to keep our end in mind. Our end is not professional success, romantic fulfillment, or self-actualization. Our end is God. Ignatius said that it is "the praise of God our Lord and the salvation of our soul." The basic idea is that we are in a relationship with a higher power who loves us and cares for us. Our end is union with God, and our decisions are means to reach that end.

The big problem is that so often we make an end out of our means. We're tempted to pursue our desires and then figure out a way to invest them with spiritual significance. As Ignatius put it: "Those [persons] do not go straight to God, but want God to come straight to their disordered tendencies." The goals become wealth, success, acclaim, and an attractive spouse. Deeper, more meaningful ends take on lesser importance—we're willing to pursue them once we build the career and find the compatible spouse. Ignatius says that this is backward.

The Gospel story of Martha and Mary is about this very thing. The two women were Jesus' friends. When he came to visit, Martha busied herself with the details of housekeeping and cooking while Mary sat with Jesus and listened to him. Jesus chided the busy Martha: "You are anxious and worried about many things. There is need of only one thing. Mary has chosen the better part and it will not be taken from her" (Luke 10:38–42). The one thing needed is to deepen one's relationship with Jesus—God incarnate. Ignatius put it a little differently. He said that the one thing is "praise, reverence and service of God." We would likely describe our end in different language, but the basic idea is that our end is union with this God. Once we focus our attention on that, everything else can fall into place.

Sometimes we think that the one necessary thing conflicts with our deepest desires. We get the idea that praising, reverencing, and serving God is something radically different from our current state. For example, a woman with a rewarding career who is drawn to marriage and family might get the idea that what God really wants is for her to quit her job, decide to be single, and work with homeless people in another state. However, Ignatius would have her ask herself whether her career and the prospect of family life stimulate more "praise, reverence and service of God." She would ask herself: "Do I do this work cheerfully? Am I more caring and loving as a result? Do I feel faith in God increasing and praise flowing more naturally?" If so, this is a clear indication that she is on the right track. This choice helps her "attain the end for which she was created."

The movie *Chariots of Fire* memorably portrays a man who knows that he must understand his truest self to choose rightly. In the movie, Eric Liddell is a devout Christian who wants to compete as an Olympic athlete. Many of his Christian friends think that competitive running is a waste of time, but Eric sees it differently. "God made me fast, and when I run, I feel His pleasure," he says. He runs to please God. That's his one motivation. When running threatens his relationship with God, Eric withdraws from a race. Eric's character is contrasted with that of Harold Abraham, another great runner, who sees athletic success as a way to gain respect in society. For Harold, "the one thing necessary," in Ignatius's words, is to win the race at all costs. Harold wins the race in the end, but the movie invites us to ask whether his motives truly brought him happiness.

Recall the decision facing Wendy, the medical student we met in the first chapter who is preparing for a career in substance abuse treatment. Wendy is also in love with Robert, and she wonders whether a life with Robert might conflict with her career. Clarity about the one necessary thing might well help Wendy see whether either or both of these possibilities are moving her in the direction of the one thing that is necessary. From what we have seen, it seems that a career in substance abuse treatment might well spring from a desire to serve God and fulfill her truest self. Her relationship with Robert, who mainly wants to get rich, might stand in the way of that.

Of course, we do not really know Wendy or Robert. Wendy may well decide that she is not as certain about her end as she thought she was. She may find that her desire to serve poor addicts is not entirely selfless but is driven by a longing to have others admire her. She may decide that her deepest desire is to be married and have a family, with professional work playing a subordinate role. In any case, Wendy's challenge is to be clear about "the end for which she is created," as Ignatius put it. This is the "one thing necessary." When she really experiences the deep love that God has for her and is able to see herself with that same love, other decisions will fall into place.

WHAT DISCERNMENT ISN'T

"The one thing necessary" helps us in several ways. It not only puts the most important question at the forefront. It also helps us understand what Ignatian discernment is all about. If our fundamental desire is to love God and respond to God's call, then the process of making choices will run along certain channels and will take on a certain character. It helps us understand discernment better by telling us what it's not.

It isn't a choice between good and evil.

Discernment is for people who have committed themselves to pursuing the good. It's not for people who are deceiving family and friends, entangled in petty crime, engaged in malicious behavior, or otherwise walking on the dark side. Ignatian discernment is useful for making choices between two or more good alternatives. It's irrelevant (or even harmful) for people who aren't sure whether they want the good at all.

Consider someone like Craig, for example. Craig is a mildly depressed young man trying to figure out what he should do with his life. He thinks that he might want to quit his job and go to graduate school. It turns out that Craig is working hard to maintain relationships with three girlfriends without any of them knowing about the others. He's drinking too much. Life has become uncomfortable at work because coworkers suspect, correctly, that he's been spreading malicious gossip about them. Craig doesn't need discernment to help him settle on a different career. He needs to make a fundamental decision to live with integrity. He needs to

choose the good, to turn away from malice and stop deceiving others. Someone might help Craig by telling him plainly
that his life is on the wrong track and won't get better until
he makes some big changes.

That's not to say that we need to lead perfectly righteous
lives to use the tools of discernment. We will always fall short
of perfection, will always encounter pride, envy, and laziness,
when we examine our feelings about the choices before us.
In fact, using the tools of discernment with discipline and
honesty may well make us *more* aware of these things. But
these defects won't hinder our discernment if our lives are
fundamentally oriented toward God. If we're not pursuing
the good, discernment won't help.

It isn't alienating.

We've already discussed the mistaken notion that God's
perfect plan is something radically different from what we
are already doing—often something radically difficult and
unpleasant. This way of thinking has its roots in a certain
kind of severe spirituality. Most religions greatly value the
virtues of austerity and sacrifice. They honor saints and holy
people who have performed great acts of renunciation; have
turned their backs on worldly comforts; and have sought God
in the desert, the monastery, and among the beggars and the
dying. This kind of heroic virtue can be seen as the ideal. It
gives rise to the feeling that God wants us to make a radical,
daunting change, and that if we follow a path that is pleasing
and satisfying to us we are settling for second best. Perhaps
there was a touch of this attitude in the case of Jon, the
young man we met in the first chapter who went to Africa
to work with AIDS patients when he decided he needed a

change. It was a bad choice, largely because little in Jon's life prepared him for such a radical change.

If we love God first, God will point us in a direction that is consistent with our deepest desires. God's desire for us will integrate well with our gifts and loves. Often, in making the right choice, we discover gifts and loves we didn't yet know we possessed. In the course of our relationship with God, we will get to know more about God and more about ourselves. It's a process of becoming the persons we are meant to be. This relationship with God may take us to surprising places, but these will not be places that are repugnant to us or that alienate us from ourselves.

This is one of the many lessons about discernment that Ignatius learned through personal experience. For a time he practiced the most severe ascetic spirituality. He prayed for hours every day, fasted heroically, let his hair and nails grow, and inflicted punishing penances on himself. The result was disastrous. He was tormented by terrible scruples and deep depression—to the point where he was afflicted by thoughts of suicide. Ignatius eventually realized that these radically exacting spiritual practices led to spiritual ruin rather than spiritual growth. He became an advocate of a balanced way of life—normal eating and workable prayer times consistent with one's work in the world.

Mortifications and penances have their place. They free us and strengthen our willpower so that we might more easily pursue the end for which we are created. But they are not the end in themselves. The one necessary thing is that we praise, reverence, and serve God. This should be consistent with our deepest desires; it should not make us miserable. As Psalm 51 says, "For you do not desire sacrifice." What God does desire is "a broken, humbled heart" (Psalm 51:19) and that our "joy might be complete" (John 15:11).

It isn't decoding secret messages.

Sometimes people think discernment is a mysterious process of reading the signs or deciphering a code: God scatters a bunch of clues, and discernment helps us read them and solve the mystery.

There are three problems with this idea. First, it suggests that God hides things from us and enjoys making decisions difficult for us. Admittedly, it is often difficult to discern God's presence; that's why we have rules for discernment. That's why you're reading this book. But the problems are our divided hearts, our pride, our desire to have it all, and our ability to delude ourselves. Many of these messages come from our culture. These messages, not God, make it harder to find the end we seek. Discernment helps us come to grips with such obstacles and determine the course of action that truly satisfies us. It's not a way to solve a mystery posed by an elusive God.

The second problem is that the notion of decoding a puzzle is a very linear concept of discernment. We start at point A, launching a process of discernment whereby we read tea leaves and chicken entrails, decode secret messages, and decipher clues. We move to point B, where we choose point C or point D on the decision tree, depending on our analysis. Eventually, we arrive at a conclusion. It can be frustrating to aim for a model of discernment like this, because in real life we sometimes go over the same ground more than once, and we only slowly appreciate the deepening significance of some of the factors involved.

What is more, and this is the third problem, placing too much emphasis on coming to a final conclusion can obscure the one thing necessary: our relationship with God. Our culture encourages us to solve our problems and reach a kind of success, after which we're all set—we don't depend on anyone, and we can just sit in our hot tub, sip margaritas, and enjoy the good life.

God invites us to a much more dynamic relationship, one that is ever deepening and in which we are constantly learning more about ourselves and others and God. God is not opposed to hot tubs and margaritas, but real life is much richer. As the saying goes, life is not a problem to be solved but a mystery to be lived.

A geometrical image that captures this better than straight lines is a spiral. We do go over the same ground sometimes, but if we are open to God, we can go deeper rather than back-and-forth. It is more a pattern of dancing together than of pacing alone.

WHAT DISCERNMENT IS

We've looked at what discernment isn't; now let's define what it is. The meaning of *discernment* is a bit hard to pin down. Like *spirituality*, *discernment* is a term that's tossed around freely to refer to different things. The term originated in the context of sorting through, or discerning, the various feelings that occur when we are in the process of making a decision. Here we will use a more popular sense of the term, which refers to the broader decision-making process.

Here's a working definition: *discernment of God's will is the act of distinguishing between options while consciously calling on God for assistance.*

It's practical.

Discernment is something that involves the concrete circumstances of daily life. Discernment is about a choice that needs to be made between options that are real possibilities. It's not about vague longings or nebulous dreams.

It's personal.

Our definition presumes that we'll get an answer. *God touches us personally.* God doesn't talk in broad generalities or lay down rules that everyone has to conform to. Discernment is practical and personalized.

It's dynamic.

When we say that discernment involves "consciously calling on God for assistance," we mean that the process of discernment is essentially a dynamic one. It involves a relationship with God, with the world around us, with the people around us, and ultimately with ourselves. The rhythm of this relationship is call-and-response; God invites, we answer. Decision-making can be compared to the back-and-forth call-and-response music of a gospel choir.

The price of admission to this gospel concert is a desire to choose the best of a number of good options. That's the one necessary thing.

SIMPLE DOESN'T MEAN EASY

The one necessary thing simplifies the way we think about discernment. But it isn't as easy as it sounds. It's not a warm and fuzzy notion of being a good person who prays and is nice to other people. Putting God first is quite demanding. It's a simple idea but a difficult one to implement.

Many of the meditations that Ignatius included in the *Spiritual Exercises* are intended to challenge the ideas we have grown comfortable with. One of the most thought provoking is an exercise that raises the question, How free are we to follow God?

Ignatius poses this situation: Three men have each acquired a fortune. All three are good people who want to serve God. All three recognize that the fortune they own brings difficulties. The money threatens to control their lives. They are enticed by the wealth, drawn to it, and tempted to organize their lives around it. All three men resolve not to let their fortune get in the way of what God wants of them. Ignatius invites us to reflect on the different ways these men relate to the problem.

The first man is all talk and no action. He acknowledges that the fortune stands between him and God. He talks a great deal about how he wants to be free. He considers many ways that he might loosen the hold the money has on him. But he never does anything about it. When he dies, he is still thinking about making a larger place for God in his life.

The second man does all kinds of things to relate more deeply to God. He prays more, he works harder at doing good for other people, he gives money away to the poor and needy. He might even use his fortune to set up a charitable foundation. But he retains control. This man would be sure to make himself the chair of the foundation's board of directors. He's serving God on his terms. He is negotiating with God. He won't do the one necessary thing, which is to face up to the hold this fortune has on him.

The third man resolves to follow God wherever he leads. To do so, he needs to be completely free, so he decides to detach himself from his fortune—"to rid himself of it so that he has even no liking for it, to keep the fortune or not to keep it," as Ignatius wrote. Note that this third man does not assume that God wants him to give his fortune away. The point of the parable is having the freedom to follow God wherever he leads. Ignatius put it this way (quoting from David Fleming's modern paraphrase of the Spiritual Exercises):

> In everyday life, then, we must hold ourselves in balance before all created gifts insofar as we have a choice and are not bound by some responsibility. We should not fix our desires on health or sickness, wealth or poverty, success or failure, a long life or short one. For everything has the potential of calling forth in us a more loving response to our life forever with God.
>
> Our only desire and our one choice should be this: I want and I choose what better leads to the deepening of God's life in me.

In other words, the goal is to be free—free at last! We can realize our deepest desires when we're disentangled from the fears and hesitations and qualms that hold us back from surrendering to the God who loves us. Achieving this freedom is a process. All we need at the beginning is a desire to be free.

That is the one necessary thing to deal with the problem of our divided hearts. Once we desire to be free, we can move on to the next job: to understand the meaning behind the conflict in our hearts.

CHAPTER 5

Making Sense of Inner Spiritual Movements

A desire to love and serve God is the one necessary thing, but it's not the only thing. It's really just the beginning. Now comes the work of dealing with our divided hearts.

Long ago, St. Augustine wrote: "Our hearts are restless, and they will not rest until they rest in You." That experience of a restless heart is universal. Every human being who has ever lived has experienced an inner struggle, a push and pull in the longing for something more. This maelstrom of emotions has many causes. Some of this is simply caused by our immediate circumstances—our own fatigue, our family genetics, and our unique personalities. But there's more. We humans are spirit wedded to flesh. Spiritual forces are at work in our divided hearts.

Ignatius was a soldier, and so it was only natural that he would describe this inner struggle as a battle. Ignatius believed that God is constantly inviting us into a deeper union with the divine. He also believed that contrary spiritual forces are constantly pulling us away from God.

Here is the battle: to surrender to God's grace or to be pulled toward darkness. Ignatius called the force that draws us toward God the "Good Spirit." He called that which pulls us away the "evil spirit" or "the enemy of our human nature."

ARE GOOD AND EVIL SPIRITS REALLY REAL?

Ignatius wrote during the sixteenth century, and thus he did not use the language and concepts of modern psychology. He did not describe our inner turmoil in terms of conscious and unconscious motivation welling up in our libido or arising from our id. But he was a shrewd observer of human nature and a passionate, practical researcher into the realm of spiritual experience. He observed the reality of our divided hearts. He knew about spiritual conflict intimately, and he used the language of spirits to describe it.

People today are all over the map on the question of good and evil spirits. Some dismiss talk of angels and devils as superstitious nonsense. Some see demons everywhere. Modern popular culture certainly seems comfortable with the idea that spiritual realms of good and evil are real. Certainly all religions of the world rest on the premise that we human beings can know something of the divine because God chooses to reveal it to us. Christian teaching is quite clear that good and evil spirits are at war in creation and in every human heart.

Are there personal good and evil spirits? Jesus believed in them. So did Ignatius and a host of other spiritual masters. So do the authors of this book. If this kind of talk makes you uncomfortable, it might help to think of the Good Spirit and the evil spirit as personifications of large spiritual forces. But make no mistake; spiritual conflict is real.

We will look at three dimensions of our spiritual experience. First is the inner conflict we experience. Second, we consider the way we are influenced by society and culture. Finally, we look at how spiritual forces fit into the picture.

GOLLUM AND THE CONFLICT IN OUR HEARTS

The first dimension of spiritual experience is simply the spiritual reality of what's going on inside us. With the gift of free will comes the ability to choose good or evil. Most of the misery in the world stems from free human choices. We've all felt the impulse to choose something other than the good. Jesus taught us to pray, "Thy Kingdom come, Thy will be done." Sometimes we live that prayer, and other times we simply want what we want without caring about God. We don't need to look outside ourselves to recognize that within us are the voice of conscience and the voice of rebellion. There are parts of ourselves that are self-destructive. As the Bible says, they lead to a kind of spiritual death (see Deuteronomy 30:15–20; Wisdom 1:1–15).

A wonderful cinematic depiction of this is found in the character Gollum in the film trilogy *The Lord of the Rings*, based on the novels by J. R. R. Tolkien. Gollum has degenerated into a piteous creature through his possession of a magical ring that destroys all who use it. Gollum agrees to help his pure-hearted master, Frodo, find his way to the fire where the ring can be destroyed once and for all. But Gollum struggles with his decision. One unforgettable scene shows Gollum arguing with himself, one moment speaking from the part of him that wants to do good and the next moment speaking from the part of him that wants to do evil.

This conflict is written in the heart. St. Paul cried out, in Romans 7: "What I do, I do not understand. For I do not do what I want, but I do what I hate. . . . For I do not do the good I want, but I do the evil I do not want. . . . Miserable one that I am!"

There are plenty of examples of this inner division found in everyday life. Susan, a college professor, is a gifted teacher who loves her students. She spends much time with them outside of class. Year after year, students rate her the most popular and effective teacher on campus. But Susan is insensitive and unforgiving to everyone else. She is harshly critical of the university administration. She dislikes her colleagues, who, not surprisingly, find her difficult and thus avoid her.

Mike is a brilliant, hard-working software engineer who gets along well at home and at work—until he explodes in anger. Rage will suddenly overtake him. He can't predict when it will happen. When fury flares up, he gives into it even though he knows he shouldn't. "I seem like a different person," he says.

Mike and Susan illustrate something we know well. We may not choose the good even though we know what it is. Within all of us is an inner struggle with those parts of our spirit that are good and those parts of ourselves that are self-destructive or evil.

THE CULTURE OF DEATH

We live in a world that is similarly divided. The cultural forces in our world influence our choices for good or ill. In his encyclical letter *Evangelium Vitae* (*The Gospel of Life*),

Pope John Paul II spoke of a "culture of death." By this, he meant negative social forces that originate in individual acts and personal sins. These forces exist within our families, our friendships, our corporations, our government, and our church. Sin is social as well as personal. In his letter *Reconciliatio et Paenitentia* (*Reconciliation and Penance*), the pope said that individuals "may be conditioned, incited and influenced by numerous and powerful external factors." In that sense, it is accurate to speak of "social sin."

The point is made in the first book of the Bible. Chapter 3 of the book of Genesis tells the story of Adam and Eve, who each personally chose to disobey God and eat of the forbidden fruit. However, Genesis 11 tells the story of the entire community rebelling against God in a vain attempt to "make a name for" themselves. God punishes this arrogance with a confusion of language at the tower of Babel.

Sinful structures abound in our culture today. Bob is a faithful member of a prayer group. He is known to others as a man of great virtue. But Bob struggles with a secret addiction to pornography. He would not have nearly as much trouble if pornography was not so easily available on the Internet. For Bob, the Internet is a powerful social influence that causes him great trouble.

Another example of societal influences for better or for ill comes from the political history of the state of Illinois, which proudly boasts "Land of Lincoln" on its license plates. The state is home to the president who freed the slaves and to our country's first African American president. But Illinois is also home to a long tradition of political corruption. This climate of corruption transcends any one individual, yet influences all those who live there. Four of the last six governors have been indicted, two have gone to prison, and another has been removed from office.

Everyone breathes the same air. When the air is pure, we flourish. When the air is polluted, we are in danger.

STRUGGLE IN THE SPIRITUAL REALM

The third dimension of inner conflict is the spiritual realm. Spiritual powers are at work, and they influence our decisions for better or worse.

Jesus saw spiritual powers at work when he asked his disciples the question we all must answer: "Who do you say I am?" Peter speaks up, stating, "You are the Messiah, the Son of the living God." Jesus replies, "Blessed are you, Simon son of Jonah. For flesh and blood has not revealed this to you, but my heavenly Father" (Matthew 16:16–17). In other words, Peter knows Jesus' true identity through the work of the Holy Spirit.

But then Peter goes on to argue with Jesus about the suffering that Jesus predicts is coming for him. Jesus sharply rebukes Peter, stating, "Get behind me, Satan. . . . You are thinking not as God does, but as human beings do" (Matthew 16:23). Jesus doesn't mean that Peter has literally turned into the devil, but that Satan is now speaking through Peter.

St. Paul called evil spirits "principalities and powers." Although this text has been misused to condone violence in the name of religion, it still offers important insights:

> Put on the armor of God so that you may be able
> to stand firm against the tactics of the devil. For
> our struggle is not with flesh and blood but with
> the principalities, with the powers, with the

world rulers of this present darkness, with the evil
spirits in the heavens. (Ephesians 6:11–12)

A biological example may be helpful here. In ages past,
bacteria were unknown. People attributed sickness to fate,
unbalanced humors, or the action of the gods. Today we
understand that bacteria are all around us, attacking our
bodies, and that we have an immune system built into our
bodies to protect us from bacteria's effects. Our understanding of this microscopic battle helps us to fight disease.

In the same way, there is an unseen spiritual battle
going on within us, a struggle for the health of our soul.
Understanding something of this battle can be very helpful
in maintaining our spiritual health.

TWO BIG WORDS: *CONSOLATION* AND *DESOLATION*

How are we to make sense of this inner spiritual turmoil?
How can it possibly be helpful in making decisions? Here is
where the Ignatian tradition has much to offer.

First, the Ignatian tradition helps us understand the inner
life by providing a vocabulary with which to talk about it.
Ignatius took the maelstrom of our feelings and emotions
and classified them into two broad categories. One he called
"consolation." This describes feelings that move us toward
God and others. Consolation is any felt increase in faith,
hope, and love that leads to a holy peace. It is commonly
experienced as feelings of peace, serenity, and joy. But consolation also includes feelings of sadness about circumstances
and personal shortcomings as long as these lead to a resolve
to draw closer to God.

The other category of feelings is "desolation." This is the opposite of consolation. That is, desolation is anything that takes us away from love of God and others. It is commonly experienced as a troubled spirit: anxiety, restlessness, doubt, upset. It sometimes includes feelings of pride and smugness about a life centered on pleasure. One of the surest signs of desolation is spiritual lethargy. Typically, a person in desolation is not naturally inclined to pray. God seems nowhere to be found, and it's not worth the trouble to try to establish contact.

Consolation and *desolation* are somewhat old-fashioned words coined in a previous era of spiritual writing, but they are really quite familiar emotional states. Nearly five hundred years of Ignatian discernment and spiritual direction haven't produced language that describes these states any better. Consolation and desolation are not rarefied spiritual states of bliss and despair. They are feelings—and the thoughts connected to feelings—that we experience all the time in the midst of daily life.

We can identify these states by looking at where they are pointing. True consolation points toward God and other people. We are happy, joyous, and at peace because we are joined with others. Our work is bearing fruit. Our family is happy. Desolation points us away from God. We're unhappy because our desires are thwarted. People don't respect us. We're all alone in a cruel world.

Consolation feels like coming home. Desolation feels like having lost our way home. Home is where we belong. It's where God is. It's where we find our right place in the human community. It's where we find the answer to the question, What do I really want?

Reflection on our emotions can thus become a trustworthy tool for making decisions. Generally speaking, consolation is the work of the Holy Spirit and desolation the work of the evil spirit. We want to make decisions associated with consolation. This is something of an oversimplification—discernment of spirits is tricky business, as we will see in the next chapter. But the language of consolation and desolation is extraordinarily helpful. It makes our emotional life part of our decision making.

HOW TO FEEL OUR FEELINGS: THE EXAMEN

Getting in touch with our feelings can be a challenge. Again, the Ignatian tradition includes a very effective tool for helping us identify our feelings and the spiritual struggle behind them: "the Examen." This practice is a way of paying attention to our spiritual experience so that we can be aware of God's action in our lives.

The Examen occupies a place of special importance for those of us working in the tradition of Ignatian spirituality. We take our cue from Ignatius himself, who regarded the Examen as the one indispensible form of prayer. He said that busy people who find it very difficult to find time to pray should always find some time to pray the Examen. The Examen has taken many forms over the centuries. The approach we like best has five points. This description of it owes much to Dennis Hamm, SJ, of Creighton University.

Begin by praying for light.

We recognize that we will never be able to see the truth of our lives without help from God. We begin the Examen by humbly asking God for the grace to see clearly. We want to get past our own thinking and desires, and to see with God's eyes. We want to want what God wants in our lives.

This is prayer with humility. We need help understanding the deeper truth of our life. To begin by praying for light is always the first step toward making a good decision.

Pray in thanksgiving.

This may sound deceptively easy, but if we've had a hard day, it can be very difficult to focus on the reasons we are grateful to God. This step is important because it puts our problems in perspective. Many of us have a tendency to exaggerate the difficulties in our lives and to dwell on the negative.

Beginning with thanksgiving puts things in perspective. No day is so bad that it can't get worse! We begin by recognizing that God is blessing us in good times and in hard times. Through all the movements of our hearts and minds and through all the activities of our day, God is calling us to greater life. Begin by thanking God for these blessings.

Be honest. Mention what you are truly grateful for, not what you think you *should* be grateful for. Of course you should be grateful for your children, but if your children are driving you crazy today, thank God for a soft chair or a quiet corner of the house.

The point is not to lie or to try to butter up God but to find the interior places where true thanksgiving resides.

Review the emotions of the day.

Every day is filled with events and encounters and thoughts that trigger emotions. Reflect on these feelings. The feelings are more important for discernment than the events that cause them. How did you react to that comment, that memo, that idea, that view of the sunset on your commute home?

Let the Holy Spirit guide you in these reflections. Nothing is so small that it's insignificant. Someone's thoughtless remark can cut more deeply and stay with us longer than an outright attack. Look at both positive and negative emotions. Look at the joy and the happiness, the laughter and the love. Look at the sorrow and the anger, the jealousy and the sadness.

Choose one of these emotions and pray from it.

Now, choose one of these feelings and probe it deeply. Experience it. Pray from it. Praying from your emotions means allowing the emotion to become your input in a conversation with God. For example, "God, I feel very lonely today," or even, "God, I'm really angry today, and in fact, I think I'm mad at you."

You might choose the strongest emotion of the day. Or you might choose the emotion that you most want to avoid exploring. You might find yourself dealing with several emotions clustered together like grapes on a vine. Be as honest as possible with God. Name the feeling as specifically as you can, and tell it to God.

After you've said all that you want to say, be quiet and listen to God's response. You may feel a stirring in your heart, or a picture may pop into your mind, or you may suddenly remember a forgotten memory. You may hear a word or phrase in your imagination. You may hear or sense nothing at all. Whatever you sense or don't sense, trust that your prayer is heard and that God is sending you the grace you need to face this situation.

Look forward to tomorrow.

This last step in Ignatius's Examen is about looking ahead. What are the lessons learned that better equip us to face tomorrow? This is about fanning the flame of faith so that we can believe that God's help will come to us each and every day. This is the assurance God offers St. Paul: "My grace is sufficient for you" (2 Corinthians 12:9).

Cardinal Joseph Bernardin, the former archbishop of Chicago, used to make it his daily practice to do an Examen. He once told a group of priests that he felt this practice was particularly helpful to him because he was a bit of a worrier. The Examen helped him realize that 90 percent of what he worried about never happened, and for the 10 percent that did happen, he was always given the grace to cope.

Practicing the Examen is a necessary prelude to making good decisions. It sharpens our awareness of the inner movements of our hearts. It builds confidence in prayer, and it strengthens humility in acknowledging our sin and weakness. This practice fortifies our trust to face the future free from fear.

Regular practice of the Examen will make us more aware of the ebb and flow of consolation and desolation in our spirits. This makes us ready for discernment. That's what we turn to next.

CHAPTER 6

Ignatius's Rules for Discernment of Spirits

Charlie is doing just fine in his busy career and active service in the community. His problem is the nagging feeling that he should be doing something different. It won't go away.

On her bad days, Anne is sure she made a terrible decision when she quit a good job and enrolled in graduate school. On her good days she thinks she did the right thing. She is seldom happy and the radical shifts in her emotions trouble her greatly.

Jon realizes that his decision to work with a non-profit in Africa was foolish and impulsive. Back in the United States, he is confused and depressed about his next step. He doesn't trust his own thinking. In fact, he thinks there might be something wrong with his mind.

Ignatius of Loyola was a widely read person, and he had an advanced degree from the best university in the world at the time, the University of Paris. But his greatest skill was the ability to closely observe and interpret what was going on in people like Charlie, Anne, and Jon. He became intimately acquainted with hundreds of them. He paid attention to the inner motions of their hearts (as well as his own). This vast practical experience is the basis for his "rules for discernment," which summarize what he learned about the spiritual meaning of our inner lives.

These rules have proven to be very useful for people making decisions, but they have broader application as well. For Ignatius, the ebb and flow of spiritual consolation and desolation were windows into the action of God. He believed very strongly that God is constantly trying to draw each of us closer into friendship. Ignatius believed that this divine movement can be seen very clearly in the "heart"—the deepest part of our selves, where emotions, will, and reason come together.

A key biblical source of Ignatius's rules is a passage from St. Paul's letter to the Galatians (5:16–21):

> I say, then: live by the Spirit, and you will certainly not gratify the desire of the flesh. For the flesh has desires against the Spirit, and the Spirit against the flesh; these are opposed to each other, so that you may not do what you want. But if you are guided by the Spirit, you are not under the law.
>
> Now the works of the flesh are obvious: immorality, impurity, licentiousness, idolatry, sorcery, hatreds, rivalry, jealousy, outbursts of fury, acts of selfishness, dissensions, factions, occasions of envy, drinking bouts, orgies, and the like. I warn

you, as I warned you before, that those who do such things will not inherit the kingdom of God.

In contrast, the fruit of the Spirit is love, joy, peace, patience, kindness, generosity, faithfulness, gentleness, self-control. Against such there is no law.

Paul says that a struggle between the good spirit and the bad spirit is being waged in every human heart. The outcome of this struggle is ultimately seen in actions—the "works of the flesh" and the "fruit of the Spirit." What Ignatius does is take a close look at the struggle itself. His rules for discernment provide criteria to recognize when the Holy Spirit genuinely guides us and when the evil spirit has deceived us.

The rules help us in four ways. They help us become aware of our inner life. They help us understand what the movements of our inner life mean, where they come from, and where they are leading us. They help us judge the right course of action by indicating which alternative leads us closer to God. They help us know how to act in times of consolation and desolation.

Ignatius wrote two sets of rules. The first set of fourteen rules applies to basic discernment; they are for people who are just beginning to recognize the influence of the different spirits on their decision making. A second set of eight rules helps more experienced people deal with the subtler influences of the spirits.

SET 1: THE BASICS

The first four rules in set 1 lay out the basic ideas of discernment. They stress the fundamental importance of one's spiritual orientation ("the one thing necessary"), and they describe the states of spiritual consolation and desolation that are the focus of discernment.

Rule 1: This is how spirits work in a spiritually regressing person.

The evil spirit attacks the good. For someone who is regressing spiritually, or moving away from God, the evil spirit will reinforce this condition. It will make evil appear to be good. It will encourage destructive, self-centered behavior by telling us that it's appealing and right. The good spirit does just the opposite with a spiritually regressing person. It will stir up unpleasant feelings, raise doubts, and sting the conscience. The goal is to encourage the person to change course.

Rule 2: This is how spirits work in a spiritually maturing person.

The spirits operate in the opposite way in someone who is moving toward God. The evil spirit attempts to knock us off course by harassing us with anxiety, sadness, and doubts. The good spirit reinforces our direction by giving us feelings of peace, assurance, and joy.

The word *devil* comes from the Greek word *diablos*, which means "the accuser" or "slanderer." The word *Satan* comes also from the Hebrew word *satan*, which means "the adversary" or "the plotter." Accusing, slandering, plotting—those are the signs of the evil spirit, which works to separate us from others and from God. It throws our faults, our failings, and our sins in our face in an attempt to discourage us. The Holy Spirit is our advocate and consoler. This good spirit encourages and strengthens us, inspires us, and fills us with peace.

Rules 1 and 2 introduce the first complication in discernment. Feelings of peace and satisfaction are not always from God, and feelings of distress and anxious doubt are not always the work of the evil spirit. The way the spirits work depends on our spiritual orientation.

To further complicate matters, no one's spiritual orientation is entirely open to God or entirely attached to evil. We are nearly always making progress in some areas and sliding backward in others. The spirits operate in different ways in the same person and at the same time, depending on the virtue or defect at hand.

> Carmen is the executive director of a nonprofit clinic that provides free medical services to the poor. As a Christian, Carmen does her work because she feels that God has called her to it. She is deeply committed to it; she finds it personally satisfying and socially constructive. But she is a demanding boss who is frequently harsh with her subordinates. She is also fiercely aggressive with local politicians and she nurses deep resentments over political battles she has lost.

For Carmen, the good spirit is likely to stir positive feelings about her work with the poor. At the same time, it may stir feelings of unhappiness and distress when she thinks about her relationships with her staff and with local political leaders whose support she needs. The evil spirit will work in the opposite way, telling her that she should be making more money in another job, and that she is right to treat her lazy and careless subordinates harshly, because that's the only way to get them to do their work properly.

We all have a mixture of selfless and selfish motives similar to those of Carmen. This mixture makes discernment tricky. We need to look at ourselves carefully and honestly when attempting to detect the spiritual meaning of our feelings. More about that later.

Ignatius wrote his rules for discernment for people whose fundamental spiritual orientation was toward God. A desire to choose the good predominates over lapses, weaknesses, and character defects. He assumed that this would be the case for anyone interested in discernment, and we assume that this is the case with you. But keep the challenge in mind. Identifying the work of spirits is no simple task.

Rule 3: Ignatius describes consolation.

Ignatius' third rule describes the state of consolation. We have already described consolation in chapter 5. (See pages 61-63.) Briefly, consolation is any felt increase in faith, hope, or love and all interior joy that leads to a holy peace.

Rule 4: Ignatius describes desolation.

The fourth rule describes desolation, which we also discussed earlier (pages 61-63). Desolation is the opposite of consolation. It tends to reinforce feelings and thoughts that take us away from God. Where spiritual consolation makes it easier to have faith, hope, and love, spiritual desolation tends to involve a decrease in these same virtues.

Rule 5: When in desolation, don't change anything you've already decided.

When we are in desolation, we are in a state of pain and God seems distant. Our natural tendency is to want to do something, anything, to get out of that state. We'd rather not turn to God in our pain. But Ignatius wisely counsels us not to run from the pain. We're to hold steady to the decisions that we made earlier when we were in a state of relative peace. Why? *Because desolation is the worst possible time to make an important decision.* We are confused, anxious, and hurting. We have no perspective on our condition. We are likely to bolt rather than to carefully assess the situation. At such a time, we don't have the freedom to make a judgment. We're in the dark, and stumbling around in the dark is a good way to fall.

Wait for the desolation to pass before making a decision. We can see more clearly when we are calm and filled with God's peace.

Good counsel for Anne, the unhappy MFA student in Iowa, would be to put aside any notion of quitting graduate school while she is in turmoil. Her decision to return to school was well considered. She made it during a time of emotional equilibrium, and she felt a deep sense of peace about it. Perhaps it was not the best decision. It's possible that she should reopen the question. But Anne should wait for a calmer time to consider whether to do that. Meanwhile, she should continue her studies; she might want to work even harder at them. Other good suggestions would be for her to accept her feelings of turmoil and pray more, to reach out to friends, to trust in God one day at a time, and to be patient and remind herself that her time of desolation will eventually pass. She would do well to practice the next rule as well.

Rule 6: Don't be passive in desolation; counterattack.

Lethargy often sets in when we are in desolation. Sometimes we are depressed. We feel helpless. We sit and do nothing except daydream about what might be or might have been. Or we engage in things that dull the pain, like turning to unhealthy substances or activities (like alcohol, drugs, food, gambling, or spending) to give ourselves a high. These things do not work because they help us run from the pain rather than deal with it.

Passivity isn't simply a symptom of desolation. It *is* desolation. Ignatius counsels us to take direct aim at these passive impulses by getting active. He suggests praying more, gently but firmly examining our consciences, training our bodies, and doing good works for other people. When in desolation, do whatever it takes to get your mind off yourself.

Spiritual desolation is not the same as depression. Depression is a psychological state that can accompany spiritual desolation, but they do not necessarily go together. A person can experience both spiritual desolation and depression at the same time, but eventually the desolation will lift, leaving the depression to be dealt with.

Characteristics of desolation. Desolation usually relates to a person's relationship with God and the struggle resulting from a loss of consolation. The root cause of desolation is temptation. Desolation usually extinguishes hope—or threatens to do so.

Characteristics of depression. In depression, the complaint usually revolves around the image a person has of him- or herself. The root cause of depression lies in a person's subconscious, in certain mental and emotional patterns. Depression can make a person listless and apathetic, as desolation does, and hope may or may not be present. Most depressed persons also struggle with hope, for often depressed people are also desolate people. William Lynch counsels the depressed to use their imagination to picture creatively how things might improve. Sometimes, however, there is a graced sense that God loves and cares for us even in our depression—a sense that motivates us to deal with the psychological depression.

Clinical depression calls for specific help. It's important to note that clinical depression often is rooted in a chemical imbalance. There are usually identifiable signs that accompany clinical depression: abrupt changes in appetite and sleep patterns, decreased ability to concentrate, listlessness, loss of sexual desire, feelings of hopelessness, and thoughts of suicide. This condition requires a visit to a physician who is qualified to make a diagnosis and go on from there.

Sam was devastated when Sally broke off their engagement. They shared a strong religious faith, had many common interests, and cared deeply for each other. Yet Sam's bouts of heavy drinking and his love for betting at the casinos disturbed Sally to the point that she decided she couldn't live with it. Sam's first reaction was to curse God and Sally. He sank into self-pity and lethargy. He drank and gambled. But being a man of faith, Sam began to face his dark side. He decided that he wanted to try to win back Sally's love and confidence. He increased his daily prayer, began to fast, started attending Alcoholics Anonymous meetings, and ceased his gambling. The verdict is still out on Sally's decision, but Sam is moving ahead by making positive choices in his life.

Rule 7: We're not on our own. God is always with us.

In desolation we feel alone. It seems as if God has departed on a long vacation. We feel miserable and unworthy, so we isolate ourselves from others and are not inclined to bother God with our prayers. Worst of all, we think that we're on our own. If anything is to be done about our situation, it's up to us to do it. Yet we don't have any idea what to do.

Ignatius reminds us that God is always there for us, even when we don't feel a divine presence. It's like the Gospel story of the storm at sea while Jesus is asleep in the back of the boat. The disciples panic and fear that they are sinking. When they awaken Jesus, he calms the storm and rebukes them for forgetting that he was always there (Mark 4:35–41).

When our storms rage, we need to remind ourselves that God is with us. We're well advised to seek out others who will remind us of that, too.

> Mary Ellen is accustomed to being alone, but she knows herself well enough to know that too much solitude is dangerous for her. When she gets lonely she gets depressed. That often leads to overeating, solitary drinking, and other destructive habits. To counter this, she deliberately reaches out to friends when she feels lonely and afraid, even when she doesn't feel like doing so. She has posted a list of her friends' phone numbers on her refrigerator. She hung a picture in her bedroom of Jesus calming the storm to remind herself of his steadfast, loving presence.

Rule 8: Be patient; desolation will pass.

Another key virtue to cultivate during desolation is patience. This may be the most important attitude of all. Desolation is not forever (even though, in our lethargy, it seems like a permanent state). Ignatius counsels us to "wait upon the Lord." The storms will eventually blow over. While they are raging, we can patiently wait for a change while we are staying active, praying more, serving other people, and doing all the other things that foster a healthy spiritual life.

> *Steve was let go from his job after working for nine years as an international business consultant. He and his wife have simplified their comfortable lifestyle while he searches for a new job. But Steve's biggest problem has been his restless anxiety. He had been accustomed to a fast-paced life of hard work and international travel. Now he sits at home, surfing the Internet for job leads and waiting for answers to his phone calls and e-mail. When he tries to pray, his prayers seem to fall on deaf ears. He feels abandoned and let down by God during this time of crisis. His wife wisely counsels him toward patience and more prayer. With some hesitation, Steve starts to pray the rosary, which he finds brings him much peace. He and his wife decide to start praying as a family and to more actively support each other in their search for God's will in their lives.*

Rule 9: Identify the cause of desolation.

Sometimes desolation seems to come from nowhere. It arrives suddenly, as if someone pulled down the window shades on a sunny afternoon. But sometimes desolation has a cause. We can learn something important by examining the cause of desolation.

Ignatius suggests three reasons. First, we might have done something to bring it on. Perhaps we neglected some important responsibilities—gave into a selfish desire, indulged the fault of someone else, grew weak and tepid in our spiritual life. If so, we can learn to do things differently.

Second, God never causes desolation, but God might be allowing the desolation as a trial so that we can grow in virtue and learn to love God and others in bad times as well as good. Consider the virtues suggested by Ignatius in the earlier rules: patience, trust, increased prayer, more service to others. If desolation causes us to grow in these ways, it's an opportunity not to be missed.

Finally, desolation may come upon us to remind us of a spiritual truth that is very easy to forget—that God is the source of everything. All is gift. We want consolation, and we will have it in due course. But we need to understand that we are not entitled to consolation and cannot obtain it through our own efforts. So we open our hands to receive whatever God gives us in the moment.

> *Jon, our friend who is mired in desolation after a disastrous sojourn in Africa, decided to combat his sadness by praying more and practicing patience. But he also carefully examined the cause of his gloomy state. He realized that his decision to go to Africa was impulsive and mistaken. He asked God to show him why he had acted impulsively. This led Jon into a fruitful assessment of his character defects— and his strengths.*

The next two rules shift gears a bit and talk about what to do during consolation.

Rule 10: Enjoy consolation while it lasts.

In times of consolation we're tempted to think that the good times will last forever (just as we think that bad times will never end). Ignatius reminds us that consolation will come and go. He prudently suggests that we store up the graces of consolation for use when times get harder, as they surely will. Establish solid habits of prayer and generous service during consolation so that you can stick to them when you are tempted to let them go. Remember what consolation is like so that you won't forget it later.

> Mike has taken this advice to heart. He keeps a journal of his prayers and reflections and is especially diligent about recording his joys and blessings. When times of desolation come, he turns to his journal and reviews what he has written about his graces. This helps him build his confidence in God's love when times are hard.

Rule 11: Remember that all our gifts come from God, and grow in humility.

Consolation is a time to thank God for the bounty we experience. We can do nothing without God. This sentiment is well expressed in a line from a song from the musical *Godspell*: "All good gifts around us, are sent from heaven above, then thank the Lord for all his love."

> Dorothy Day, the cofounder of the Catholic Worker movement, made a fundamental decision to live forever close to the poor. Living out the consequences of that decision was often difficult. One chilly day in London, she picked up some newspapers off the street and used them to line her thin coat. She said to her friend Eileen Eagan, "I thank the men of Skid Row for teaching me this way of keeping warm." Wherever she was, Dorothy always found a reason

> *to be grateful. It is no surprise that the two words carved on her gravestone in Staten Island are* Deo Gratias *(thanks be to God!)*

The last three of the fourteen basic rules elaborate on points made in the earlier rules. Ignatius shifts his method of teaching and offers metaphors to get his ideas across. The evil spirit is like a bully, a false lover, and a military commander.

Rule 12: Resist the bully and face it head on.

The evil spirit is like spoiled children or bullies. If you give them what they want, they will only demand more and more. Seeing your weakness, they will grow stronger. Instead, be firm. Stand up to their taunts.

It often requires courage to stand firm. If we keep running from our fear or our addictions or our sin, we will never get away. As the psychologist Carl Jung said, we need to get our shadow out in front of us.

> *Tony is a man who came to his spiritual director acknowledging that he had been promiscuous and unprotected in his sexual activity. He feared that he might be HIV positive, and yet his fear kept him from going to see a doctor. He thought it was easier to live with not knowing than facing the possibility of being overwhelmed with the knowledge that he might have HIV. He felt frightened, powerless, and discouraged. In working with his spiritual director, he saw the importance of stepping into the light, facing his fears, and arming himself with the knowledge of what he would have to face. He began to pray with greater fortitude and perseverance. He did go to the doctor, and even when his fears were confirmed, his*

faith continued to sustain him in the long and difficult struggle that lay ahead.

Rule 13: Tell someone; resist the urge to keep problems secret.

The evil spirit is like a false lover who demands that the liaison be kept secret. This allows the affair to continue unchecked. The evil spirit is like mold. It thrives in the dark. Ignatius urges us to let God's love shine on our lives. We can do this by making our fears and temptations known. The evil spirit causes us to be fearful about telling others what we are struggling with. Resist that fear. Share your problems and fears with a counselor, a spiritual director, a confessor, or a trusted friend. Prudence demands that we choose our counselors wisely.

A central step in twelve-step recovery programs is step 5—a full disclosure of one's past to a trusted adviser. It's no surprise that the twelve-step movement draws heavily on Ignatian spirituality.

Opening up to someone else made all the difference for Tom, a professional church worker who has served people splendidly over the years. He has been married for more than a dozen years, but the flame of passion in his relationship with his wife has grown quite dim. He began an affair with a woman whom he met at a church event. The excitement, the pleasure, and sense of fulfillment seemed unbounded. The fact that he met this woman at church appeared to be a sign that God blessed his renewed passion. Tom wisely brought this affair into the light by talking to his spiritual director about it. As he genuinely sought God's will, Tom was able to distinguish the superficial consolation of the affair from the subtler grace calling him back to fidelity in his marriage. Tom courageously made the decision to break off the liaison and recommit to his marriage. With counseling and a lot of hard work, his marriage now is strong and healthy.

Rule 14: Know your weak points and strengthen them.

The evil spirit is like a military commander looking for weak spots in the enemy's defenses. That's where the military commander will attack. To counter, look for your weaknesses and shore them up. Self-knowledge and humility are key in resisting attack. The prouder we are, the more vulnerable we are to being blindsided by our weakness.

Mary is a single woman in her late fifties who spent more than a decade of her life caring for her aging mother. When her mother died, she was hit with overwhelming sadness and loss. She quickly decided to sell her house and move to get away from the painful memories that surrounded her. She thought that God wanted her to do this. But Mary also knew that she was prone to black-and-white thinking—judging situations as wholly good or wholly bad without making subtle distinctions. This made her prone to dramatic, sudden decisions that often didn't turn out well.

Mary wisely pulled back and discussed her situation with a trusted friend. In the conversation, she was able to see something that she could not see by herself—that she was in a time of depression and spiritual desolation. She decided to wait until her mind and emotions were settled before deciding whether to sell her house.

These fourteen rules provide a firm foundation for discernment. But there's more. The work of spirits is often subtle, especially in the lives of people who know enough to spot an overt assault, as in the case of the military commander. For these more complex situations, Ignatius has a second set of rules.

CHAPTER 7

Rules for Subtle Discernment

Most decisions involve choices among two or more plausible, possible, worthy options. At least this is the case for people who have rejected wrongdoing. The question is, Which is the best choice? Ignatius's second set of rules for discernment is especially helpful here. All of our options will be appealing to some degree. These eight rules help us discern when the appeal is genuine and when it gets us off track. The rules mainly deal with false consolation, which is the work of the evil spirit disguised as something good.

Rule 1: A general principle about the work of spirits.

For those bent on choosing the good, the work of the evil spirit is likely to be subtle. It will more often take the form of doubts and dissatisfaction than despair and open defiance. It will try to deflect us from the best course of action through distraction, discouragement, and doubts.

Jim is a basketball coach who recently converted to Christianity after having been raised without any formal religion at home. Jim is very attached to his church. His friends are important supports as he grows in a life of prayer, Scripture reading, and service. Lately, Jim has been experiencing a deeply felt sense of Jesus' love for him. He has been trusting God's faithfulness and has been amazed at how this trust has brought peace and new relationships into his life.

Jim has received a job offer from a university in another state. The job is an excellent opportunity—it's exactly what he has been working toward during the past five years. All the signs in his discernment point toward accepting the position. Yet Jim is burdened by doubts. It would mean giving up everything that is familiar to him. He especially fears leaving his church community. He doubts that he could ever find such a strong Christian community in his new city. He fears losing his faith. Shouldn't fears about his faith be taken seriously? Aren't such fears from God?

But when Jim prays, he feels a still small voice encouraging him to trust that God will be waiting for him in the new city, just as God is present where Jim is now. Jim comes to see that his fears and doubts are a spiritual attack from the evil spirit cleverly disguised as a reasonable concern for his Christian faith. The quiet voice of assurance and confidence is the voice of the good spirit.

It's often hard to see the truth about such spiritual attacks when we're in the midst of the struggle. A wise friend, mentor, or spiritual director can help us sift through such fears and worries so that we can discern the leading of the good spirit.

Rule 2: Feelings of consolation with no apparent cause are from God.

Usually feelings of consolation have a cause: experiencing success in our work, having a good time with someone who loves us, enjoying a splendid work of art. But sometimes they seem to have no cause. A joyful peace descends suddenly. Love for God and gratitude for God's gifts bloom in our heart for no apparent reason. We can be confident that these feelings of consolation with no apparent cause are from God.

> Michelle is a microbiologist who was sitting in her research lab and looking at cell samples a week after her father's death. Her life seemed out of focus, her work dull, her prayer dry, her heart stunned by the loss of a man she loved so well. As she peered into her microscope, she was suddenly flooded with all the memories of her father's love. His gentle smile, his quirky sense of humor, his habit of teasing her about her freckles, and his encouraging her to follow her heart's desire to become a scientist.
>
> She felt a great peace come over her, a sense that her father was at rest and that she could face her future with hope once again. This consolation without any previous cause came at a time when she really needed this gift. She can trust that it is from God.

The remaining six rules involve discerning false consolation. These are feelings of joy, elation, peace, and confidence that may originate with the evil spirit or be exploited by it.

Rule 3: Don't assume that feelings of consolation with a cause are from God.

We need to be cautious when we can readily identify the cause of our spiritual feelings of consolation. They may be from the good spirit, or they may not be. The evil spirit can use this consolation to distract us, focus us on ourselves, and puff us up with pride at our good deeds or holy thoughts. This was how the evil spirit disturbed Walt.

> Walt is an architect who inherited a family-owned firm from his father. A year after his father's death, Walt sold the firm and made a small fortune in the process. Walt was delighted; he gave thanks to God. He also decided that the surprising success of the deal showed that he was a pretty smart business-person as well as a good architect. He took great pleasure recalling the way he had negotiated the deal. Soon he was thinking grandly about other projects he could undertake. He grew annoyed with people who showed insufficient enthusiasm for his ideas. He felt that others didn't appreciate his talents. Why couldn't everyone see that God had blessed him with keen insight well beyond that of the average man? Walt's business colleagues began avoiding him. His wife told him that he was becoming irritable. His children wondered why their father had been so critical of them lately.

Walt's delight has an easily identifiable cause: his profitable (and surprising) business deal. But the evil spirit used it to tempt Walt into pride. He forgot that he was first and last an ordinary human being.

Rule 4: For someone seeking the good, the evil spirit usually appears as an angel of light.

The evil spirit isn't stupid. A person set on choosing the good should be able to see and resist an outright spiritual attack. Thus, the evil spirit will disguise itself as an angel of light. For example, we can be deflected from the right course by irrelevant thoughts of some other good thing we might do. Or we can be tempted to take pride in our accomplishments and good deeds, thinking that we alone are responsible for them. An attack disguised as a spiritual benefit or worthy motive can become a Trojan horse. We let down our defenses and welcome the evil spirit into our home, where it can wreak havoc on our souls.

> Claire, a recently married young woman, is dissatis-
> fied with her job at a small nonprofit social service
> agency. She's considering a job change or perhaps
> going back to school. She asks for prayers about the
> situation at a prayer group she has belonged to for
> many years. After one meeting, she talks about her
> problem with Eric, a young, attractive single man
> who has also been part of the group for a long time.
> She and Eric pray about her job situation. During
> the prayer, Claire is struck by a strong feeling that
> she has broken through into a new love for God. It
> becomes quite clear to her that God is calling her to
> go back to graduate school.
> Claire excitedly calls Eric the next day to discuss
> this prayer. She feels that Eric has special wisdom
> for her. She thinks that God has brought Eric into

her life in answer to her prayer. They talk several times in the next week. As she seeks confirmation of this decision, her mind keeps returning to Eric, the strength of his hands, the warmth of his smile, the fragrance of his cologne.

Claire is heading down a dangerous path. It's a good idea to seek direction from God about her future, but it's not a good idea for a married woman to seek this direction through a close personal relationship with an unmarried man. Notice how Claire's attention shifts away from God and onto Eric. The notion that Eric is a special envoy from God is likely a temptation from the enemy. It's an attack cleverly disguised as something spiritually beneficial.

Rule 5: Review a consolation carefully to determine its nature.

Look at the beginning, middle, and end of a spiritual consolation to determine whether it comes from God. How did it start? How did it develop? Where has it left you now? If it began well and has left you focused on God, you can be confident that God is behind it. If it began well but now you find yourself doubtful or fearful or self-absorbed, you should suspect the influence of the evil spirit.

Joe is a workaholic who teaches at a local community college. He works twice as many hours as his colleagues, has trouble setting limits, and often gets inappropriately involved in the work of others at school. He has been accused of not respecting boundaries. And when he overworks he gets crabby and hard to live with.

Joe knows this about himself so he decides to do something about it. He cuts back on the hours he spends at work and begins to go to the local YMCA gym for some long-neglected exercise. At the Y he plays pick-up basketball with teens and young adults. This leads to an invitation to coach one of the teams in the Y's youth basketball league. Flattered, Joe accepts. The team does well. Joe then accepts an invitation to join the board. Then he becomes chair of the fundraising committee. Relishing the responsibility and enjoying the attention he receives, Joe throws himself into the work. Soon he is neglecting his teaching and his family to pursue the new volunteer work. Eventually, it all comes crashing down. Joe gets burned out, becomes depressed and discouraged, and quits volunteering completely.

Joe's project began well but it got off track. The evil spirit was able to exploit Joe's tendency to work too much by manipulating the joy and satisfaction that volunteer work gave him. It not only harmed Joe but also deprived a good organization of an effective volunteer.

Rule 6: Learn from mistakes.

When you have been deceived by a false consolation, find out why and how it happened. Review how it unfolded. Find out where you got off track, and resolve to improve. God is not judgmental. God doesn't affix blame but invites us to keep paying attention and to keep learning from past mistakes.

In the first chapter of this book, we met Charlotte, the retired educational software designer who suddenly accepted a demanding dream job when a former colleague offered it to her over the phone. "I felt like God himself was giving me this job," she told her appalled husband and friends. It soon became clear that Charlotte had made a mistake. She didn't really have the energy or desire to do the new job, and she turned it down. Charlotte used this embarrassing situation to learn about herself. Why had she reacted so impulsively? Was she dissatisfied with her life in retirement? Should she be doing other things?

Ignatius insisted on a daily Examen because it heightens our ability to reflect on our experience. "Those who ignore history are bound to repeat the past," goes the proverb. The same is true in the spiritual life for each of us. Only by prayerfully reflecting on our experience will we be able to learn from our mistakes.

Rule 7: The feeling of the consolation is a key to its source.

The good spirit is gentle as God is gentle; the evil spirit is noisy and disturbing. Ignatius uses images to explain this. The action of the Holy Spirit is like a drop of water hitting a sponge or like walking through an open door into a house. Our hearts are the sponge or the house. They are ready to receive God's grace, which enters peacefully. By contrast, the work of the evil spirit is like a drop of water hitting a stone or someone banging on a locked door trying to get into the house. It's disruptive, harsh, and loud.

Look at the tone and feeling of a spiritual movement. If it's an appealing idea that leads to turmoil and anxiety, it may not be from God. If it's an idea that fills you with tranquillity, it may be from the good spirit.

Charlotte reflected at length about her life. When she retired at age fifty-five, she had felt some pangs of guilt at giving up a rewarding and lucrative professional career. Those feelings never went away. She had been one of the first women to achieve success in her field, and she felt that walking away from it was somehow weak—something that a man wouldn't do. She wondered what younger women thought of her.

Going back to work was a real option for Charlotte, but it seemed like something she should do. However, she genuinely enjoyed her busy life in retirement—volunteering at a hospice, working in community organizations, and spending lots of time with her children and grandchildren. She had freely chosen to stop working so that she could do those things. By contrast, the idea of going back to work was burdened with feelings of obligation and guilt. The "feeling" was all wrong. Those harsh feelings did not seem trustworthy.

Tiffany had an experience similar to Charlotte's as she was deciding between marriage and religious life.

Tiffany was raised in a devout Catholic family and loved mass, retreats, and works of Christian service. She thought that God might be calling her to religious life. Tiffany also had a steady boyfriend, Tom. When she prayed about becoming a nun, she thought that she owed this to God. She felt that it was something that she had to do. In contrast, she continued to feel great joy when she thought of marrying Tom and having a family. Still she felt plagued by guilt that she wasn't being generous in her response to God.

She started spiritual direction to try to gain some clarity. Her director helped her understand that God calls us in freedom. The constant guilt and the sense of obligation to become a nun are not the marks of

the Holy Spirit. Tiffany was able to let go of her false
sense of God's call to religious life and embrace her
heart's desire of moving toward marriage with Tom.

The Examen (see chapter 5) can be a very useful tool here.
A practice of regular reflection on our spiritual lives can
help us see the qualitative differences between the way the
good spirit and the evil spirit work. That's how it worked in
Ignatius's life. The good spirit gave him lasting peace. The
evil spirit gave some initial euphoria but left him agitated
and unsatisfied. With careful reflection, we can train ourselves to notice the same sorts of qualities.

Rule 8: Don't make a quick decision in the afterglow of a consolation from God.

Consolation is one thing—the warm glow following consolation is something else. It is entirely possible to receive a consolation from God and then go on to make a bad decision. The
afterglow of the consolation can blind us to the faulty reasoning we might use to do something we selfishly want to do.

On a pilgrimage to Italy while visiting the tomb of
St. Francis of Assisi, Nathan experienced one of the
most powerful encounters with Christ he had ever
known. His heart felt like it would burst from the
love of God he now felt. Upon returning home, he
announced to his wife that he thought they should
sell their comfortable home and move to a poorer
neighborhood, stop teaching religious education
to children, and start ministering to the homeless.
When his wife wisely suggested that they take
some time to pray about these things, he became

*agitated and accused her of being selfish and mired
in material comfort.*

Nathan was failing to distinguish a genuine consolation from its afterglow. His consolation called for some kind of a response, but he needs to more carefully discern what it might be. We need to use all the tools of discernment to make good decisions. That's what the rest of this book is about.

Two Important Ideas from the Second Set of Rules

The eight rules for subtle discernment contain some of Ignatius's most acute and useful observations about the spiritual realities of our inner life. They are especially relevant because they are directed at people who have already made a fundamental decision to choose the good. If you are sincerely trying to do the right thing, then you are well advised to pay special attention to these rules. Two ideas of special importance stand out.

First, the work of the evil spirit in your life is likely to be subtle. You will seldom be tempted to do something overtly sinful; rather, the temptations will be disguised as something good. You will become distracted, lose your focus, wander into fretting and worries. You will be tempted to do too much or to act too soon.

Often the temptation is to see ourselves as God's gift to humanity. The evil spirit will have us become too generous by working inhumane hours, become too much of a perfectionist by developing standards of excellence that ignore how God often works through human imperfection, become too helpful by not delegating or allowing others to collaborate with us, or become too eager to manipulate situations that are not quite ripe in God's grace. In short, we will be tempted to run ahead of God's grace. This is the central temptation that Jesus experienced in the wilderness (Luke 4:1–13).

The second idea follows directly from the first: we almost always need help discerning subtle spiritual movements. We are well advised to call on a wise friend, mentor, or spiritual director for help in discerning these movements. The evil spirit wants us to forget that we are fallible, limited human beings; sharing our decisions with another person will keep us grounded in reality.

CHAPTER 8

Five Pillars
for Sound Decision
Making

Our decision-making tool kit is filling up with advice, principles, observations, wise insights, and sensible attitudes. We are about ready to move on to the three modes or methods for actually making decisions in the Ignatian tradition. But first we should spend a little more time on five principles that we have found to be especially important. Think of them as pillars holding up the roof of a good decision. They stand on the foundation of love of God and the vital interior freedom needed to make a good decision.

These five pillars have to do with discernment of spirits, a reflective mind-set, the importance of emotional calm, getting help from others, and the use of the imagination. We've touched on all of them. Here we'd like to say a bit more about them.

1. MAKE DISCERNMENT OF SPIRITS A PRIORITY

A good decision involves some measure of prayerful and reflective assessment of inner spiritual movements. We typically discern this by looking at the part of our personality that involves the emotions. Modern psychology calls this the affective part of our personality. It is every bit as important as our reason and our will (our cognitive and conative faculties, as psychologists call them). This does not mean that we simply go with the choice that feels right. Nor does it mean that decision making is always a prolonged process of introspection and analysis of the subtleties of our emotions. A good decision involves all of our faculties, including reason and will. But one of the great insights of the Ignatian tradition—some say the greatest insight—is that our emotions are trustworthy indicators of God's presence. A decision made in the Ignatian mode almost always includes the deep-down feeling that the choice is right.

That's because we find God in the deepest recesses of our hearts. The heart is the place where reason, will, and emotion come together. As we will see, each of the three modes of Ignatian decision making emphasizes one of these faculties. But all three are necessary. Of the three, the realm of feeling is perhaps the most difficult to assess and understand. That means that the greatest rewards are often gained by paying proper attention to it. That's what Ignatius's rules for discernment equip us to do.

The question to be constantly asked in decision making is, *What do I really want?* Deep down, that's what God wants, too. God wants what is best for us. This isn't something repugnant or burdensome or sad or difficult. The way of life that God desires for us is the way of life we desire. *What do I really want?* is a simple question, but simple isn't the same as easy. Usually this question is quite difficult to answer. Our deepest desires are obscured by pride, fears, ambitions, and attachments to money, honor, security, and a host of other things. The process of discernment is essentially a process of stripping away these false desires and finding the desires at the core of our selves. Discernment of spirits is a way of grasping what these deep desires are.

The path is a spiral into deepening awareness. You feel your way along the path. You reflect on the choices before you and observe how they affect you. In which direction do they take you—toward the trinity of Father, Son, and Spirit, or toward the trinity of me, myself, and I? How do you feel about your choices? Observe the feelings. Time goes by sluggishly when you think about alternative A; time speeds up with reflection on alternative B. Choice A makes you feel restless, upset, discontented; it raises more questions. Choice B seems to fit better. A turns you in on yourself; B seems to point you toward others. These are the kinds of movements we observe in ourselves when we are discerning spirits.

2. SPEND TIME IN PRAYERFUL REFLECTION

It seems obvious that discerning a decision requires periods of quiet reflection. But we will say it anyway: *You need to spend time alone in quiet prayer and reflection to hear what's going on inside.* And we don't mean twenty minutes mulling things over while you're out for a walk or driving to work. Serious reflection needs periods of solitude. You need enough quiet time for the buzzing in your head to subside so that you can hear what your heart is saying.

It's often a challenge to simply become *aware* of feelings. We can go through a day of frustrations, accomplishments, boredom, and achievement without being very much aware of the emotions connected to these events. We push the feelings to the edge of our consciousness and press ahead with the duties of the day. Such stoic detachment can help us preserve mental equilibrium in the face of life's pressures, but it's no use at all when we're trying to interpret our feelings. The first step is often to sit down in a quiet place and allow ourselves to *feel*.

The next step is to make this a habit. Good decisions are the fruit of a reflective cast of mind. The daily Examen is an excellent way to cultivate this habit of calm reflection that allows us to truly feel.

3. DON'T ACT IMPULSIVELY

Someone offers you a fabulous job with twice the salary you were expecting. The partner of your dreams unexpectedly proposes marriage. A can't-miss investment opportunity comes your way. The Ignatian approach (and common sense) tells you to wait until the euphoria has passed and then take a sober look at the decision you are facing. Even more common is the urge to do something when you are feeling bad. The partner of your dreams dumps you. You feel weary, oppressed, and sad at work. You're bogged down in graduate school; you can't get the new business off the ground; the new volunteer service is full of frustration. At times like these, we're tempted to make a change to make the bad feelings go away.

Maybe you should. But maybe you shouldn't. You are not likely to know as long as you are feeling anxious and miserable. One of the most important principles in Ignatian decision making is never to make a decision when you are in a time of desolation. Wait for a time of tranquillity. Get some distance from the feelings of confusion and anxiety, and discern what they mean.

A common mistake—one made even by spiritually mature people—is to assume that desolation is always bad. It's true that the aim of discernment is to make choices that are associated with feelings of consolation and that our choices will bring us greater peace and joy if we are growing in our relationship with God. But feelings of desolation often have an important role in the process of decision making. Desolation can be an opportunity for positive change. Pain can spur us to seek God more eagerly. Feelings of desolation are not in themselves destructive. What is hazardous is to change a decision while under the influence of these feelings. Steve's job crisis is a good example of this point.

Steve is a man in his forties who had left a teaching career to become a social worker. He took a job in a large university hospital and after a year became overwhelmed by feelings of weariness and disappointment. The work itself was difficult, but Steve's main problem was with his colleagues. His boss was cold and critical. The social workers were divided into factions and were in constant conflict with one another and with other departments of the hospital. Steve distanced himself from the political rivalries, but this caused his colleagues to resent him.

When Steve realized that he was going to work every day in an angry and resentful frame of mind, he thought it was time for a change. He knew a little about discernment. He thought he should probably return to teaching because he felt much better when he imagined himself back in the classroom. The signs seemed pretty clear. Social work meant desolation. Teaching meant consolation.

Steve came to see that discernment was more complicated when he took the matter to his spiritual director. Yes, his desolate feelings at work pointed toward the need to make a change. But what kind of change? Had he made a big mistake when he left teaching for social work? Perhaps, but that had been a carefully considered decision, and it seemed unwise to reverse it while he was feeling miserable about his job. Other possibilities presented themselves. Could Steve change the way he related to his coworkers and his boss? Perhaps he should look for another job as a social worker. Perhaps he had to adjust an exalted and unrealistic idea of what it meant to be in the helping professions. Steve decided not to make a hasty decision. It would take some time—and some calm reflection—to determine what his desolation meant.

A word of caution: sometimes it's necessary to act quickly without waiting for a calm time for reflection. (In particular, someone in an abusive relationship should leave immediately if he or she is in danger). We often have to make immediate decisions about medical treatment, family crises, problems on the job, and other situations on a tight deadline. In these situations, do your best and trust that God will be with you.

4. Talk to a Trusted Counselor

Steve's job crisis illustrates another important principle of decision making: don't keep it to yourself. Steve needed help to see that there was much more at stake in his job problems than he thought. So it is with everyone. Good decision making is a process that involves other people.

Ignatius felt strongly about this, so strongly that he said that the impulse to keep a decision a secret from others is a sure sign that the evil spirit is at work. Time after time, he observed decisions going awry when people cut others out of the process and set forth on their own. One of his rules is to involve others in our choices. This is especially important when we are experiencing desolation. We can get into deep trouble when we don't tell anyone about the pain we are suffering.

Talking to a wise friend makes good practical sense. We might overlook something, and it's always helpful to have a sounding board. But the most compelling reason to seek assistance is a spiritual one. Decision making is inherently collaborative; its goal is growth in relationship with God. Reaching this goal involves a relationship with others. Discernment is not meant to be a solitary activity—we don't do it for ourselves, and we don't do it alone. A crucial part of the process is sharing it with a wise and trusted counselor or friend.

5. Use Your Imagination

The fifth pillar for sound decision making is creative use of the imagination. This does not mean daydreaming about a perfect world or wishful thinking about something that isn't likely to happen. Imaginative exercises in the Ignatian mode are disciplined, focused reflections on our choices. They can help elicit the feelings of consolation and desolation that are the raw material for discernment. They can clarify our reasoning. The imagination is an especially useful tool when we don't seem to be making progress. These exercises are worth trying even if they seem odd or uncomfortable.

Ignatius employed several imaginative exercises to help in decision making. Try them when you've identified your alternatives.

What would you say to someone else?

Go to a quiet place, put a chair in front of you, and imagine yourself talking to another person who is facing the same decision you are facing. You have never met this person before so you can be objective about his or her predicament. At the same time, you genuinely like this person and want to be of help. Carry on a conversation. Listen to the way your imaginary companion describes the situation. What questions would you ask? What does the person say in reply?

Imagine the conversation as vividly as you can. Consider the gestures and body language, tone of voice, subtle signals. What might the person be unaware of? What more would you like to know about the situation? Listen carefully to what you say to this person and then apply this advice to yourself.

Try it on for size.

Choose one of your alternatives and spend the next few days imagining that you are living your life in this way. Then take the other alternative and spend a few days living it out.

Again, let your imagination go. Imagine the choice vividly. If you are someone like Steve, the unhappy social worker, you might imagine that you have already made the change and become a teacher. What is your day like? You get up early and commute to work. You're in front of a class of students. Some want to hear from you and some don't. You are delighted at the progress some make but disappointed at the performance of others. You spend more time than you like at home correcting papers and preparing lesson plans. You meet with parents. You are frustrated by your work on a committee that makes fitful progress toward revising the curriculum. A former student drops by to thank you for how well you prepared him or her for college. How does all this feel?

Alternatively, you might imagine that you have not made a change but have decided to stay in your job with some adjustments. Imagine what that's like. You are Steve back in the hospital social work office. You've adjusted expectations. This job is far from perfect—it's not as good as some but better than most. You reach out to resentful colleagues with small acts of kindness. You do your best to understand what your boss wants and do it. You focus on serving patients and their families. You think about the satisfactions of helping them and less about gossip and political machinations in the department. Results are mixed. How does that feel?

Note the feelings associated with these alternatives. Do you feel more joy and energy imagining one way of life? Does one make you feel sad and anxious? Use the methods of discernment to interpret these feelings.

Present your alternatives to a trusted friend.

Imagine bringing your choices to someone you deeply respect and trust. It could be an actual person or an ideal mentor or counselor that you conjure in your imagination. It could be Jesus. Present the choices to this person and observe how he or she reacts. How does this make you feel?

The point of this exercise is to note your feelings in response to the person's reaction. You might be surprised. Perhaps you are disappointed when the mentor approves a choice and pleased when he or she disapproves of another.

Look back from the end of your life.

Imagine that it is some years into the future: your life is drawing to a close and you are taking stock. Of the alternatives facing you now, which do you wish you had made? How did you make this decision? At the end of your life, do you wish you had made it differently?

The point of this exercise is not what-if speculation about how your life unfolded—it's to assess how you make the decision you are facing now. Looking back, what values are most important to you? Are these the values that will have guided this decision? For example, money is very much on your mind as you consider several job offers. This is a legitimate concern because your family needs an adequate, steady income. But, in the bird's-eye view of your life, how important is the difference in salary compared to other factors in the decision? Another example: you are thinking about quitting a good job and going to graduate school to prepare for a new career. You are excited about another career but worried about the impact of a drastic reduction in your household income on your spouse and three children. At the end of your life, which concern seems most important?

A famous example of this imaginative exercise involves Alfred Nobel, the Swedish inventor who endowed the Nobel Prizes. Nobel invented dynamite and made a fortune from manufacturing weapons. In 1888, a French newspaper mistakenly published a premature obituary of Nobel, which condemned him and stated that "the merchant of death is dead." This caused Nobel to take stock of his life. He resolved to leave a better legacy. When he died in 1896, he left most of his fortune to endow the prizes that bear his name.

Our decision-making tool kit is now full. It's time to study the three scenarios for Ignatian decision making.

CHAPTER 9

Decision Making
in Mode 1:
"No Doubt about It"

I gnatius thought that a decision could be made in three ways. The first method or mode is a certain conviction that leaves little room for doubt. The second mode emphasizes interpretation of states of consolation and desolation, and relies heavily on discernment of spirits. The third mode emphasizes our intellectual faculties, especially our reasoning and imagination. We'll discuss these modes in the next three chapters.

The three modes of decision making are described in the *Spiritual Exercises* and have been closely identified with the Ignatian spiritual tradition for centuries. Ignatius did not invent them; he discovered them. They are the product of years of careful observation of what actually happens when people who love the good make decisions. They are based on keen insights into human psychology and the way God actually interacts with human beings. Thus, these modes have a certain universality.

It's also true that speaking of different modes of decision making is something of an oversimplification. Apart from the first mode (God's direct intervention in a person's will), Ignatius describes two general approaches. One involves interpreting the shifting feelings of consolation and desolation that we experience as we ponder alternatives. It emphasizes the emotions. The other approach emphasizes the intellect. But the modes do not exclude each other. Ignatian decision making seeks to bring the emotions and the intellect together whenever possible. We apply our reason and knowledge to decisions, but we also listen to what our feelings say. Sometimes feelings take center stage, and sometimes they wait in the wings until the head has done the heavy work. Ignatius believed that we can accurately discern God's will when we get in touch with our deepest desires. This is the heart—the place where our emotions, thoughts, and feelings come together.

PRAYER IS THE FIRST STEP

Ignatius assumes that the person making a decision is a prayerful person. He suggests that this person pray for three things.

1. Pray for the light to make the best decision.

These methods of decision making are for people contemplating two or more good options. They are not for someone who wants to start cheating on their income tax or to get revenge on someone who has slighted him or her. We should explicitly pray to make the best decision.

2. Pray to know God's will.

God wants to be an active participant in the decision-making process. Explicitly invite God in. Pray to know God's will and to be guided by the Holy Spirit. God loves us and cares about our decisions. We can turn to God as our closest and most trusted friend.

3. Pray to be open to the options available.

We reach a good decision when we are able to pray as Jesus did: "not what I will but what you will" (Mark 14:36). Trust in God. God wants what is best for you. Practically speaking, this means that we strive to imagine ourselves living with either choice. Most of the time, we prefer one of the alternatives. That is fine as long as we can see ourselves taking the other path. Pray to reach this state of inner freedom.

FIRST MODE:
"NO DOUBT ABOUT IT"

The first mode is when God makes the decision perfectly clear. A person experiences an overwhelming certainty that one of the alternatives is the right one. There is simply no doubt about it.

In this mode, God affects the will—the part of our personality that is able to act on the decisions the mind makes. This is the mode in which God's presence is most overt and direct. God is somewhat more hidden in mode 2, which mostly involves the emotions, and is further in the background in mode 3, which emphasizes reasoning.

Ignatius cites two well-known examples of a mode 1 deci-sion in Scripture: the call of Matthew and the conversion of Paul. In the Gospel story, Jesus walks past Matthew the tax collector and calls him to follow. Matthew immediately drops everything and follows without hesitation (Matthew 9:9). The conversion of Paul is even more dramatic. Saul (who had been persecuting Christians) is knocked to the ground, given a vision of blinding light, and hears the voice of Jesus speaking to him: "Saul, Saul, why are you persecuting me?" When the bewildered man asks, "Who are you, sir?" he receives the unambiguous reply, "I am Jesus, whom you are persecuting" (Acts 9:4–5). Paul has no doubt about what he needs to do in response to this. He surrenders his life to Jesus and goes on to become the church's greatest missionary, carrying the gospel to Jews and Gentiles alike.

Another famous conversion story that's similar to Paul's is that of John Newton, the eighteenth-century author of the hymn "Amazing Grace." Newton was a slave trader. One day during a terrible storm, a man who had just taken his place on deck was swept overboard. Realizing that his own life had just been spared, Newton saw an unmistakable invitation to surrender his life to Christ and to God's amazing grace. However, Newton continued to work as a slave trader for many years before he actually surrendered his life to Christ. When he did, he became a powerful antislavery activist. He played an important role in the abolition of the slave trade in Great Britain in 1807.

Newton's story illustrates an important caution: knowing the right decision isn't the same as acting on it. Sometimes we know perfectly well what the right decision is. God has made it clear in a mode 1 fashion, leaving no doubt. But we resist it. We manufacture uncertainty. We might even under-take a discernment process to assess alternatives, knowing full well that one of the alternatives is the one God is asking of us. Consider the famous plea of St. Augustine in his *Confessions*: "Lord, make me chaste, but not yet!" He had no doubt that stopping his promiscuous behavior was the right thing to do. He just didn't want to do it.

Few of us will be invited dramatically by Jesus to follow him or be knocked to the ground and experience a blinding light, but there may be times when the right choice is unmistakably clear. Sometimes it comes from a profound experience of God's presence in our lives. Sometimes we have a gut sense of what we need to do.

Kathleen was a young architect who had dated many men. Several times she came very close to getting engaged, but she hesitated because it never felt quite right for her. Then she went through a time of personal crisis and eventually emerged from it a stronger and more faith-filled woman. Then she met Franco, a man very different from anyone she had ever dated. He was a stonemason who had never been to college. They went out on their first date, and she came home that night and told her mother, "I met the man I'm going to marry." She bided her time to confirm that her initial gut reaction was correct and in fact it never changed. A little more than a year later, they married. Eleven years and two children later, they are still very happily married. Kathleen's choice was absolutely right.

Reflecting on this, Kathleen pointed out that more than a "gut feeling" was involved in her conviction that Franco was the man for her. She was very struck by Franco's admission that he believed in God and the power of prayer. This, more than anything else, opened her to the surprising idea that they belonged together.

Indeed, a decision in the first mode is not an impulsive, unthinking decision but a surrendering to a clear movement of grace. It is a peaceful cooperating with God acting on our will.

CHAPTER 10

Decision Making
in Mode 2:
Spiritual Movements

Most of the time we are conflicted when faced with an important choice. One alternative seems attractive, but then we have doubts about it, and another alternative seems better. Misgivings creep in, and we decide that the first choice was better after all. But we're not sure. We are pulled back-and-forth.

Ignatius thought that this movement back-and-forth between consolation and desolation was the usual condition in the heart of a person trying to make a significant decision. When the matter is an important one, it stands to reason that the struggle in our conflicted hearts would intensify. The good spirit and the evil spirit are active, and their work shows up in the unrest deep within us. This is normal; in fact, Ignatius told spiritual directors to worry only when *nothing* seemed to be going on in the heart of someone facing an important decision.

Usually something is going on. This is where the rules for discernment come into play. What follows is a description of the decision-making process involving discernment of inner spiritual movements. Mode 1 decisions show God acting directly on our will. Decisions in mode 2 show God acting on our emotions. God is not as immediately present to us in mode 2 as in mode 1. But the spirit of God is present nevertheless, and we find it by examining feelings of consolation and desolation.

This description is presented as a step-by-step process. This doesn't mean that it's a linear process. As we've said many times, the course of a decision about an important matter is usually a spiral into deeper awareness of ourselves and greater love of God. We learn new things and reopen old questions. Nevertheless, the process of making a decision has a beginning, a middle, and an end. Here's a description of how it would ordinarily play out in mode 2.

1. Pray for knowledge of God's will.

You begin a mode 2 discernment by placing yourself in God's hands and asking to be guided by the Holy Spirit. Pray explicitly to know God's will.

2. Pray for freedom.

Ask for the grace to do what God wants of you, whatever that is. This is a crucial request—perhaps *the* crucial task in decision making. Can you imagine yourself taking either of the choices before you? Chances are that fears, desires, aversions, and dreams cloud your thinking about your options. You are drawn to some things and repelled by others. Much of the confusion that surrounds decision making involves the contradictions of these conflicting desires. True freedom means a firm and clear desire to do only what God wants (which is what we want in our deepest selves). It is clarity of purpose.

Becoming truly free to choose what God wants rarely comes easily. You are likely to return to this prayer for freedom often in the course of a personal discernment.

3. Notice movements of consolation and desolation.

Ask God for help in noticing the spiritual movements that have already occurred. Usually, as soon as we realize that we have to make a choice, we have some initial reactions. We might be excited about a new possibility; we might experience a wave of fear. The Examen prayer (see chapter 5) is a good tool for recalling the waves of feelings that have occurred.

4. Imagine yourself having made the decision: Try it on for size!

Tentatively choose one of the possible alternatives. Live with that decision for a while and see how it feels. Note what rises up inside you as you sit with the new decision.

Perhaps you actively picture your new life as vividly as you can. You have left the social work job and have become a teacher. What is your day like? Don't just imagine the satisfaction of helping youngsters learn new things. Also imagine correcting tests and preparing lesson plans in the evening, talking to parents, and dealing with unruly students in class. Again, the imaginative exercises described in chapter 7 are very helpful in weighing a tentative decision.

Do you feel more joy and energy imagining this way of life? Or does it make you feel sad and anxious? It's not just the feelings that arise immediately, but the subtler movements of the heart and soul in the aftermath of the decision that are particularly instructive. What is the aftertaste of the decision? In what direction do the feelings move you? Toward greater faith, hope, and love? Or more toward focusing on yourself and your own narrow needs?

Often these feelings will surface immediately. Sometimes they won't, and you will have to spend some time accessing them. You might pray the Examen prayer to help detect these feelings. Note in a journal these feelings and spiritual moments.

5. Try the other option on for size.

Now reverse the process and imagine yourself having made just the opposite decision. You've decided to stay in the social work job. You are trying to reach out to your coworkers. Several respond positively; most don't. You are trying to pay more attention to serving your clients and worrying less about gossip and political machinations. How does that feel? Step inside the inner world that this decision brings. Pay attention to the aftertaste of the decision. Note in a journal these new feelings and spiritual movements.

If the right decision is not clear, repeat the previous two steps. The more important the decision, the longer it may take to gain some clarity on the pattern of the spiritual movements arising from the consolations and desolations you experience. Review your spiritual journal and look for the pattern of consolation, of peace and tranquillity. Often the pattern will be obvious by this point.

6. Discern the source and direction of your feelings.

Spiritual consolation and spiritual desolation are not the same as feeling good or feeling bad. Many positive and negative feelings can arise in discernment that are not necessarily meaningful. For example, the prospect of the new job might excite you because it will give you the chance to travel to interesting places. It might make you sad because you will miss pleasant lunch conversations with your former colleagues. Such feelings are not entirely irrelevant. In fact, you may want to explore why you feel this way, especially if the feelings are intense. But surface feelings such as these are not usually spiritually significant.

Spiritual consolation and spiritual desolation are deeper feelings that affect our relationship with God in some way. They involve the fundamental disposition of the heart. They lead to a deep sense of rightness and wrongness. Spiritual consolation has to do with a sense that certain actions will bring us closer to God and help us more fully realize what we truly desire. Spiritual desolation is a sense that we are getting away from who we truly are. A course of action seems unwise, uncomfortable. It's alienating—it's not "me." Spiritual consolation involves the feeling of coming home. Spiritual desolation involves feeling we have lost our way home.

The evil spirit can subtly manipulate feelings of consolation to mislead us. The good spirit can help us learn from feelings of desolation to warn us of danger. The rules for discernment (chapter 6) are very helpful as we identify the spirits involved in these feelings.

7. What does this mean for your decision?

The rules for discernment are also useful for the next step: determining what the spiritual movements mean for your decision. Your goal is to find the work of the Holy Spirit. When you find yourself experiencing more true consolation in a particular decision, usually that is a sign that the decision harmonizes with God's will. If you notice that a particular decision brings you more desolation, usually that is a sign that a course of action is not God's will for you. If all goes well, one of the alternatives will emerge as the preferred one, because it is the one most strongly associated with consolation stirred up by the good spirit.

8. Discuss it with someone.

Don't do this by yourself. Find a spiritually sensitive friend or counselor who can help you look at the matter objectively. You may have overlooked something important. The very process of describing your decision to another person is likely to help you understand it.

9. Decide and seek confirmation of the decision.

Now that you have some clarity about which choice to make, take the decision to God. In the *Spiritual Exercises*, Ignatius tells us to be explicit about this. Take the decision to Christ and say, "This is what I've decided to do. What do you think?"

It's easy to skip this step. People are relieved to have made a decision, and they want to get on with it. They are sure they've made the right choice—at least they are pretty sure—and they don't want to hear anyone raising second thoughts. But confirmation is important. Present this decision to Christ. Is it the most loving thing you can do? Are you comfortable with it? Ask for a sense of confirmation. Often this will come by the gradual lifting of remaining doubts and anxieties.

HOW DOES THIS WORK
IN REAL LIFE?

This second mode of discernment comes right out of Ignatius's own conversion story. Recall that as he lay in bed recovering from his battle wounds at his family's castle in Spain, he started to read the lives of the saints. As he imagined himself imitating St. Francis and St. Dominic, he was filled with joy and a newfound desire to serve God. Yet he also fantasized about resuming his military career and romancing the princess of Spain. This also filled him with an immediate joy.

Both fantasies were tremendously appealing. Both evoked a flood of euphoric emotion. But slowly Ignatius began to recognize a difference. When he thought about returning to his military career and pursuing a romance with the princess, he felt happy. But later, as some of the feeling of sexual intrigue wore off, he felt dry, listless, and anxious.

When he meditated on the life of Christ, he was filled with a joy that melted into a lingering peace. This brought hours of deep spiritual consolation. Ignatius noted the difference and surrendered to God's grace. He chose to leave the military career and to follow Christ. As we noted earlier, this was the humble beginning of Ignatius's formulation of the second mode of decision making. Over the years, he would refine the process. But the essence of the decision making would remain the same: look for the movement of God's grace stirring your emotions to true spiritual consolation. That's the decision to make.

You may say, "That's fine for Ignatius, but what about us today?" Fair enough, let's look at three contemporary examples of people using the second mode of decision making.

Ed and Gina had both been looking for a marriage partner but couldn't find that right someone. They met each other one day in a hospital chapel, where she worked as a nurse and he volunteered praying with the sick. They dated, fell in love, and talked openly with family and friends about getting married.

But Ed was a bit older than Gina and much shyer. He was plagued with doubts and paralyzed by the fear of making a wrong decision.

Gina, in turn, wondered whether she would be accepted by Ed's close-knit, large Catholic family. Her family and friends were advising her either to move forward with the engagement or break it off and move on. She became frustrated, and their relationship began to stagnate. The longer they procrastinated, the stronger the doubt grew that they would remain together. Clearly a decision had to be made.

They were both people of deep faith, so they decided to seek spiritual counsel. Their spiritual advisor suggested that they face their doubt by applying this second mode of decision making. They committed to daily prayer for a month. During that time they agreed neither to see each other nor to have any communication between them. They followed the discernment process as outlined above, praying only for the knowledge of God's will for them and the strength to carry it out. At the end of the month, they agreed to meet independently and then together with the spiritual director to help them reflect on what they had learned in prayer.

At the end of the month, they were much relieved. They came to the joint session of spiritual direction with big smiles on their faces, for now there was no doubt. Both had received strong consolation as they imagined their married life together. Neither really wanted to live separate from the other. The agonizing fear of making a mistake was broken. They set a date for their marriage, and now, years later, Ed and Gina are happy together with their two children.

A second example comes in discerning a vocation to religious life.

> Bill was a young lawyer fresh out of law school when he decided to enter the Jesuits. His best friend told him he was throwing away his life. His father reacted angrily. Without really knowing much about the process, Bill started making a mode 2 discernment of his decision. The prospect of life as a Jesuit filled him with feelings of satisfaction and enthusiasm. Thoughts of a career as a lawyer made him anxious and unhappy. Becoming a Jesuit seemed right, but Bill wasn't sure. He wondered whether his best friend was right, and he was troubled by his father's opposition. Still, as Bill continued to pray about the decision, the scales tipped in the direction of entering the Jesuits; that was where he continued to feel consolation. He decided to enter the Jesuits, and then he prayed for confirmation of this choice. Despite the continued opposition from his father and friend, more peace flooded his heart. Some of his uncertainty continued, but he had the confirmation he needed. He said to his father, "Dad, I can give my life for you, but I cannot live my life for you."
>
> A second level of confirmation came after Bill entered the Jesuits and lived the life for a while. His feelings of peace and joy deepened. His doubts and fears dissipated. For Bill and many others, a decision is finally confirmed only after it's translated into action.

Finally, to further illustrate mode 2 discernment, let's revisit in some depth the case of Charlie, the hospital administrator we met in chapter 1 who can't shake the idea that he should undertake a different volunteer service. Let's see how Charlie might make a decision about this by discerning the spirits.

Here's Charlie's case:

> Charlie is the administrator of a large cardiovascular surgical unit at a university hospital. It's a demanding job; he routinely works fifty-hour weeks, sometimes more. A year ago, when the youngest of his three children started college, Charlie was freed up to take on some outside volunteer projects. He joined the board of a nonprofit organization that supports music education in the city's public elementary schools, with a particular focus on minorities and children of immigrants. Charlie has accomplished a great deal. He's raised a lot of money and helped recruit local musicians to volunteer their time. The program has been expanding. Charlie is very satisfied with his work. He loves music. He likes the idea of helping young people learn to love it, too.
>
> A month ago, two close friends of Charlie's asked him to join them on the board of a nonprofit organization that sponsors literacy education projects in the community. The group needs fund-raising help, some new ideas, a jolt of energy. Charlie can do all this. Charlie is immediately drawn to the idea. He thinks about it for a while, and the answer seems clear: he says no to his friends. He doesn't have the time to serve on both boards, and his work in music education has been very productive. However, the idea of literacy education won't go away. Charlie keeps thinking about the invitation. He puts it aside;

it keeps coming back. He wonders: Should I recon-
sider? Should I do this?

Decide to decide.

The first step is to decide whether any kind of a decision is necessary. Charlie's decision to work in music education had come after much thought and prayer and careful discernment. To even consider changing it, there needs to be a good reason.

Is there a good reason? After prayer and reflection, Charlie decides that there might be. The idea of shifting his energies to literacy education persists in his mind even though he has done everything to slam the door on it. He resisted the idea when it first came up (even though it intrigued him). Later he considered it more seriously and said no. But the prospect of working in the new program won't go away. Most of the time it stirs feelings of consolation. Charlie is excited by it. He decides that it's possible that the invitation from his friends to do something different might be something he should do.

Pray for freedom.

Charlie prays to be free to make the choice that God wants for him. He wants to be detached from any personal desires and interests connected to either music education or literacy so that he can see the choices clearly.

A couple of attachments surface. Charlie realizes that he is quite flattered to be asked to take on the challenge of reviving the literacy project. He enjoys listening to his friends extol his talents. He thinks they may be right when they say that he is the only guy in town who can give the program new life. He imagines himself giving banquet speeches about literacy, meeting with the governor, and helping other cities duplicate his success. These feelings contrast sharply with the frustration he's been feeling lately with progress in the music program. Fund-raising has slowed down. Charlie has talked to several wealthy potential supporters who told him that they just don't think music education is all that important.

Charlie probes these feelings. He sees a dollop of resentment and a large helping of grandiosity behind them. The wealthy donors' view that other things are more important than music education comes across as an opinion that *Charlie* is not that important. He resents the implication. Charlie also sees that much of his musing about the literacy job has to do with feeling important, needed, and acclaimed. Charlie acknowledges these self-centered feelings and asks God to remove them. He does not want these feelings to influence his decision.

Experience consolation and desolation.

Charlie now reflects on each alternative and lets feelings come to the surface. He employs imaginative exercises to stimulate his emotions. He imagines that he is giving advice to a friend who is dealing with the same issue. He meets some people involved in the literacy project and spends a day imagining what it would be like to work with them. He does the same with the music program (without the resentment). In his imagination, he brings the question to a teacher he had in college whom he loved dearly.

Are these emotions relevant to discernment?

Charlie feels many emotions during these exercises, but only some of them seem to be relevant to a spiritual discernment. Thoughts of the new job excite him, but over time the excitement subsides and is replaced by a growing sense that literacy education is where he should be devoting his energies. Charlie feels good about the music program, too, but the feelings of consolation are less powerful. They are also more diffuse; a sense of rightness is lacking. He also notices something interesting: Many of his most intense positive feelings about his music work are personal in nature. Charlie loves music. He likes to hear it. He enjoys being around musicians. By contrast, most of his positive feelings about literacy have to do with the good that an expanded, energized program could do for people, most of them poor.

What's the spiritual source of these feelings?

Charlie thinks that the consolation he feels about the literacy program is stirred by the Holy Spirit. But he's not sure. He still catches himself daydreaming about the praise that could come his way if the program succeeds. He knows that literacy is more important than music in the minds of many people he respects, and that he will appear more selfless and more socially progressive to them if he makes the switch. He worries about this. Are these feelings, which are basically positive and not without foundation, a form of false consolation from the evil spirit, designed to draw him to work that he shouldn't do? More subtly, is his worry about acclaim and prestige a form of desolation from the evil spirit intended to deflect him from deciding for the literacy program? There's more work to do.

Get help.

Charlie discusses the entire situation with his close friend Paul, a priest who once was his pastor. Paul brings up a couple of questions Charlie hadn't thought much about. Did he really know enough about the demands on his time that the literacy program would make? Charlie's wife says she will support whatever he decides to do, but has he discussed it thoroughly with her? She knows him better than anyone else. Charlie makes inquiries and talks over the matter with his wife. There seem to be no obstacles.

On the crucial question of the discernment of spirits, Paul advises Charlie to relax. He has a pretty clear answer: feelings of strong consolation caused by the good spirit are pointing toward the literacy program. The worries about grandiosity and his worries about the worries are distractions.

Make the decision.

Charlie decides to accept the invitation to join the board of the literacy program. He sits with the decision for a few days. Nothing changes in his positive feelings about it. No obstacles arise. No new reasons come forward.

Look for confirmation.

Charlie has some concerns, and he acknowledges that he isn't 100 percent sure, but deep down he is convinced that this service is the best one for him. Gradually his assurance grows. He is excited and pleased by the prospect of the new job. Charlie makes the call to accept the position.

Charlie made his decision primarily by discerning the spiritual meaning of his emotions. He did not ignore reasoning. It simply wasn't a big part of the process. The decisive factor was the way he was able to detect the presence of God in the emotions he had as he considered his alternatives.

But this doesn't happen with everyone in every situation. Some decisions don't seem to engage the emotions very intensely. In these situations, we turn to mode 3 of Ignatian decision making.

CHAPTER 11

Decision Making in Mode 3: Calm Deliberation

The third mode of decision making makes particular use of our mental capacities, especially our abilities to reason and analyze. It comes into play when our emotional state is relatively tranquil. We don't feel strong emotions of consolation and desolation when considering our alternatives. Some version of mode 3 is also useful when decisions are complex, requiring us to weigh many factors. In these situations, we find God's will through our reasoning. In mode 1, God directly affects the will. In mode 2, we discern God through our emotions. In mode 3, we use our mind to find the right path.

As always, describing a distinct mode 3 of decision making risks oversimplifying what Ignatius really meant and, indeed, what really happens. The will, emotions, and reason are always involved in any good decision. A mode 2 decision arrived at by discerning consolation and desolation always includes an element of reasoning. Feelings and emotions are part of a mode 3 decision. The ideal in the Ignatian tradition is a unity of the will, emotions, and mind. All are present in a decision. The different modes serve differences in emphasis.

Ignatius describes two versions of the mode 3 decision. One emphasizes a careful analysis of the pros and cons of one's choices. The other adds imaginative exercises to the equation. We blend the two versions into one here because, in our experience, decision making in real life usually employs both reason and imagination in the same process. We present mode 3 as a step-by-step process. This does not imply that this process is in any way mechanical or rigid—it's not even linear. As we've said before, Ignatian decision making resembles a spiral more than a straight line. It is a process of burrowing deeper into knowledge of self and love of God, and it frequently involves looping back to revisit questions that have already been partially answered.

The preparation for a mode 3 decision is the same as others. Place yourself in God's hands. Pray explicitly that you will be able to choose the most loving course of action. Ask for help and expect to receive it. We're accustomed to think *God helps those who help themselves.* But the true biblical attitude is different. Jesus said, "Ask and it will be given to you; seek and you will find; knock and the door will be opened to you" (Matthew 7:7).

1. IDENTIFY THE DECISION TO BE MADE

Mode 3 is for important decisions, not a choice about where to go for vacation or whether you should wait another year before replacing the roof on the house. Decisions like these often involve deeply entrenched values that might bear close scrutiny using some of the techniques we've described, but this mode is for major commitments that are not undertaken lightly and are not easily reversed: decisions about career, marriage, education, jobs, service work, and the like. The alternatives might be clear: to accept or decline a job offer, whether to leave an abusive marriage, whether to retire early or keep working. Often, however, the issue at stake has to be clarified. The following are some guidelines.

The issue should be practical and real.

Your decision should not be a vague idea or intention. It's a decision to do or not to do something. For example, the thought *I really should do something to get out of this dead-end job* is not an issue for a decision. A decision would be, "I am going to stay in marketing and look seriously for a new job," or "I'm going to do this [go to graduate school, take some courses, start a side business] to prepare for a different career."

The decision should be one that you have the right to make.

You can decide to seriously pursue marriage, but you can't get married until you and your partner are both in a serious relationship. You can decide to have a career in computing, but you can't decide to work for Google until Google offers you a job.

You must have the information to make an intelligent decision.

Decision making often grinds to a halt because we don't know enough about the alternatives. What salary will the new job pay? What time commitment does the volunteer opportunity really require? Often we must make a decision without all the information we would like to have. If so, we must take uncertainty into account. "Am I willing to take on the new job when I really don't know how much time it will require?"

2. State the Choice Concretely

State the question as a positive choice as concretely as you can. Be specific. Boil it down to two choices if possible.

Most choices can be stated in one of two ways: X versus non-X or X versus Y. The first kind of decision is something like "I will take a course in conversational Spanish this summer." The second kind of decision is something like "I will stay in my current job, or I will quit and start my own business."

It's often helpful to state the choice in the way that appeals to you most at this early stage of decision making. If you want to start your own business, pose the issue that way: "I will start My Graphic Design business by next July, or I won't do that." Don't be afraid to tell God what you really want.

3. Pray for Inner Freedom

Achieving true freedom is the most important step and the most difficult one. We return to it several times in the decision making process. The goal is to be free to choose the alternative that most fully expresses our deepest selves. We've reached this degree of freedom when we can sincerely imagine ourselves living with either choice. We want only to do what God wants, which is what we want in our deepest, truest self. To get to this point of freedom, we must be free of the personal attachments and desires that stand in the way.

Some of these are unspoken shoulds and oughts that narrow choices ("A good life means material comfort and a respectable job," or conversely, "A good life means being a rebel and living on the margins"). Some of the obstacles are character flaws: feelings of superiority or inferiority, a need to control everything, fierce competitiveness, self-pity, resentment. Others are desires run amok: greed, lust, power, a passion to be admired.

Take this example: A job offer comes your way. It's a challenging, well-paying job with a start-up company. You are not looking for a new job, but you consider this one. Perhaps you are someone like Charlotte, the retired software designer whom we met in the first chapter who was suddenly offered her dream job. You are powerfully attracted to the new job opportunity. Why?

Well, the new job will pay a big salary, and there's the possibility that you could get rich if the start-up is successful and purchased by a big company. This appeals to you very much. So does the idea of leaving your current job. It's a good job, and you enjoy your work, but upper management has turned down some of your pet projects lately, and you've been feeling unappreciated and a bit resentful. You would be one of the partners in the new company, with lots of control and no executive team to shoot down your good ideas. You like the image that the new job conveys to others—a bold, risk-taking entrepreneur, not a boring bureaucrat in a big company. You like the fact that success in the new job might impress your father, who has always been critical of you. Finally, you relish the idea of the impact your departure will have on your current bosses. They will be sorry to lose you and envious of your good fortune, and they'll wish they had treated you better.

There's much to sort out here. Money is important, but how important? Are you being influenced by greed? How strongly do resentment and self-pity color the way you think about your current job? How much do pride and a desire for power affect your thinking about the new opportunity? Why is your father's approval so important? Why does the prospect of your colleagues' dismay please you so much?

None of these concerns is completely dishonorable (except the pleasure you feel in others being unhappy). But your thoughts are colored by wishful thinking, fantasies, and warped desires. Most important decisions are like this. The core question is, What do I *really* want? To answer that question, we need inner freedom, and achieving inner freedom requires time, honesty, hard work, and prayer to ask God's help.

4. GATHER ALL THE NECESSARY INFORMATION

Get all the relevant facts: What? Where? When? How much? Why? Is the decision yours to make, or do others have to make decisions, too? If others are involved, have they made these decisions? Are important practical details unclear?

Consult with everyone who will be intimately affected by the decision (spouse, children, friends, colleagues). Listen to what they think, but also make careful note of how they feel. Are they agitated, enthusiastic, happy for you, worried?

Discuss the matter in detail with someone who will be honest with you and objective about the situation. Look for a spiritual counselor who knows you well enough to have an idea of your strengths and weaknesses but is not so close to you as to have a personal stake in what you decide. This person should be able to help you focus on the question, What do I really want?

5. Pray for Inner Freedom, Again

Pray about the decision again in light of what you've learned so far. Most likely new issues have arisen. Your spouse is excited about the idea, but several of your friends are negative. Someone has suggested an entirely new idea. Your spiritual director brought up several points that hadn't occurred to you previously. This has stirred up some new feelings and desires (such as disappointment, anxiety, elation). Bring them to God in prayer. Pray for freedom to make the decision objectively, influenced only by the desire to do what God wants, which is doing what you really want at the core of your true self.

Many people find it helpful at this point to pay attention to the emotions that the process has stirred up. Reflect on the feelings of consolation and desolation that you may be experiencing. You might make a commitment to praying the Examen every day while you are making this decision (see chapter 5 for more about the Examen). This will help you get in touch with the feelings and then identify the spirits that cause them.

6. Make a List

Take a sheet of paper and list all the reasons for and against each alternative.

For a proposal in the form of X versus non-X, you will have two columns in your list: advantages and disadvantages.

I will take a course in conversational Spanish next summer	
Advantages	*Disadvantages*
Spanish would be helpful in my current job.	I will have to work very hard to learn Spanish.
It's a good credential for future jobs.	The best summer course is very expensive.
It will satisfy my desire to learn something new.	I won't be able to do other things next summer.
I've always wanted to learn another language.	I might fail. I'm not very good at languages.
Having another Spanish speaker at work would serve clients better.	

For a proposal in the form of X versus Y, you will have four columns: advantages and disadvantages for each alternative.

I will stay in my current job		I will quit and start my own business	
Advantages	*Disadvantages*	*Advantages*	*Disadvantages*
I enjoy my work	It's a family business. I'd rather not work for my father and uncles.	I think I can be very successful in my own business.	It's a risk. I may fail.
I make a very good salary.	Future prospects for this business are uncertain at best.	I will be able to use all my skills and abilities.	It means long hours at work and less time for my family and work in the community.

I will stay in my current job		I will quit and start my own business	
Advantages	Disadvantages	Advantages	Disadvantages
I have time for my family and community service.	My best ideas aren't going to be implemented here.	I'll treat employees more fairly if I am in charge.	It's a big financial risk.
It will keep peace in the family.	I seem to be harboring more and more resentment against my father because I work for him.	My spouse has been urging me to do something like this for a long time.	My father and uncles will not like this at all.

List all the reasons you can think of. Work quickly. Put the reasons down as they come to you. Don't evaluate them (You'll do that next). Don't hesitate to list reasons that seem less than noble.

7. EVALUATE THE ADVANTAGES AND DISADVANTAGES

Ask God for the gift of openness and freedom, and then evaluate your list of pros and cons. Go over each reason on the list. Reflect on them; pray about them. Be mindful of how they make you feel. Be open to hearing what God says about them. The point of this evaluation is to determine which advantages and disadvantages come from the Holy Spirit and which do not. As you go over the list, ask these questions.

Which reasons seem to be the most important?

Starting your own business brings up financial security, time with your children, job satisfaction, and family peace. Which one or two of these issues strikes you as the most significant? Why?

What values emerge?

Several advantages and disadvantages may be pointing to the same value. The pros and cons of taking a conversational Spanish course might boil down to a choice between a desire to always be learning something new versus an impulse to be prudent and cautious.

Which core values seem more consistent with your true self?

Do you see yourself as a cautious person? A risk taker? Someone who is concerned about the opinions of others? Reflect on these values. What are your motives? Are you truly that kind of person?

You may have to spend a lot of time on this step. You may have to repeat earlier steps: praying for freedom or gathering information.

8. TEST YOUR REASONING WITH YOUR IMAGINATION

You've applied your intellect and reason to the task, and the reasons for preferring one option over the other are lining up. Now is the time to employ another mental faculty to test those reasons. Use your imagination. Take some time to imagine yourself living out each choice. Use the imaginative exercises described in chapter 7. Imagine that you are talking to a friend facing the same choices. Imagine that you are looking back on this moment from the end of your life. What values seem most important to you. Imagine that you are telling a wise mentor about why you have made the choice.

In mode 2, the imagination is used as a tool to stimulate feelings of consolation and desolation. That may well happen in mode 3, but the primary reason for using imagination here is to test your reasoning. Do your reasons make sense when you explain them to a mentor? Do they sound convincing when you hear an imaginary friend telling them to you? Do some reasons seem trivial and irrelevant? Do some seem especially weighty?

9. Make a Tentative Decision

God has been influencing you through this process. The Holy Spirit has touched your reasoning and shaped your desires. Now is the time to pay attention to your will—your capacity to decide. Your will has probably settled on one of the alternatives before you. If so, make a tentative decision.

Perhaps your inclinations remain unsettled and are fluctuating between two options. Ask God for clarity about them. If clarity doesn't come, pray for inner freedom again. Fluctuating, unsettled inclinations are a sign that you are being influenced by unspoken shoulds or oughts, a character flaw, or a selfish desire. Identify these obstacles and ask God to free you from them.

10. Confirm the Decision

In the Ignatian approach to decision making, confirmation of a decision usually involves feelings of spiritual consolation.

These are feelings of peace, enthusiasm, confidence, and joy. They are spiritual feelings—that is, they are not merely transitory emotions but deeper movements of the heart. They flow from a settled conviction that the chosen path is clearly pointed toward loving God, serving others, and realizing your deepest desires.

Confirming a decision involves more than the powerful feelings of consolation. Our other faculties may take the lead. Our analytical ability might confirm a tentative decision as we realize that the arguments in favor of it make more and more sense. We might experience a growing inclination to go in the direction of a tentative decision. One of the most important signs of confirmation is the lifting of fear about actually living out the tentative decision. You know that a decision to leave your job and go to graduate school is correct when you are no longer afraid of failing, going into debt, or upsetting your friends.

This step completes the integration of the whole person in the process of discernment and decision making. We've engaged our thoughts (gathering information, listing advantages and disadvantages). Our feelings are engaged as we ponder a tentative decision. Finally, as we act on a decision, our will is engaged. A decision is confirmed when all of our faculties—thoughts, will, and feelings—are aligned so that we are confident that our choice is correct.

11. MAKE YOUR DECISION EVEN IF YOU ARE NOT CERTAIN ABOUT IT

Sometimes God will confirm a decision by giving us an overwhelming, unmistakable certainty that a tentative decision is correct. But this is rare. Usually there's some uncertainty. Our thoughts, will, and feelings may all tell us that this decision is the right one, but there are no guarantees. We don't control the future. We make the best decision we can, realizing that the good things we hope will happen may not happen. They depend to a large degree on the decisions of other people and the progress of events that no one can foresee.

Knowing this, it's not unusual to hesitate at the point of making a final decision. We procrastinate, waiting for certainty.

The rule of thumb in these situations is "If there's no don't, then do." If there's no red flag in your analysis, inclinations, and feelings, then go ahead. Decide—and trust in God. The decision, important as it is, is but a step on your journey. It's means to an end; the end is God. If you keep the end in view, all will be well.

JOE PATERNO'S DECISION

Joe Paterno became head football coach at Penn State University in 1966 and had outstanding success almost immediately. His teams were among the best in the country. They went undefeated in two seasons and won three prestigious bowl games. Paterno was heralded as one of the best college coaches in the country.

In 1972, Paterno received an offer to leave Penn State and coach the New England Patriots, a struggling professional team. Paterno, who was paid a salary of $35,000, would be paid $1.3 million by the Patriots—an unheard-of sum at the time. He would also get an ownership stake in the team. Paterno considered the decision carefully. He made a list of pros and cons. He talked to colleagues and mentors. All the signs pointed toward accepting the offer. The money was very attractive. But it was also a superb career opportunity for a young coach. Paterno accepted the job verbally and made plans to fly to Boston to sign the contract. He told his wife, Sue, "Tonight you get to sleep with a millionaire."

But Joe didn't get much sleep. He lay awake thinking about his decision. He realized that what he really liked about coaching was working with young men and playing a role in their development as human beings. He saw that professional coaching could never mean what college coaching meant to him. He decided to turn down the job. In the morning he told his wife, "Last night you went to bed with a millionaire, but this morning you woke up with me."

Paterno's decision to leave Penn State seemed to make sense, but it was never confirmed. His misgivings did not go away. Instead they increased until Joe could see what he really wanted—not money and glory but the satisfaction of making a positive difference in young men's lives.

CHAPTER 12

Signs of a Good Decision

Certainty is hard to come by when making decisions. We are flawed human beings with clouded minds and restless hearts. When the moment of decision finally arrives, there will always be an element of uncertainty. We don't know for sure that this choice is perfectly right. In the end, we are trusting God, whose intentions we don't fully understand.

However, we can have a high degree of confidence that we've made a good decision. By following the principles and the process of Ignatian decision making, we can be secure in the knowledge that we've made the best effort we can to discern the right path in the circumstances we are in and with the knowledge and time available to us.

Four factors in particular are signs of good decisions. They have to do with movement, freedom, the engagement of the whole person, and deeper knowledge of the self.

A GOOD DECISION
LEADS TO MOVEMENT

A good decision causes something to change. This might seem obvious, but it's not. Often we reach a decision after a long process of reflection, but nothing happens as a result. "I will find another job . . ." "I will take an MCAT preparation class as the first step to get into medical school . . ." "I will ask Diane to marry me . . ." But these things don't happen. The resumes don't go out. The application is unsent. The question goes unasked.

Sometimes there's no movement because the choices haven't been formulated correctly at the beginning of the process. A good example is a decision to look for another job. You probably dislike some aspect of your job—everybody does. But this time, the boredom or the pressure has become so great that you decide it's time to move on. You mention this to your friends. You go online and send out some resumes. You might engage in a version of a mode 3 discernment to assess the pros and cons of staying at your job or leaving, and then you might decide to leave. But you never launch a serious job search, and six months later you're still in the same place.

Perhaps laziness is the reason. More likely, you need to learn something more about yourself before you can address the job problem. Are you afraid of making changes? Are you attached to security and prestige? Should you make changes in the way you relate to people at work instead of leaving your job? At bottom, you may not know what you really want out of life.

This problem can arise in the work of committees and groups as well. A group discusses a problem for several hours. Then, ten minutes before the meeting ends, the chair says,

"Okay, let's make a decision," and a decision is made. But nothing comes of it. No one takes the initiative to implement the decision, or implementation is halted when the first difficulty is encountered. This is a sign that a decision was not really made. The issues were not discussed thoroughly enough, objections didn't surface, and the decision made at the end of the meeting was passive assent that lacked real conviction.

Some assistance from the outside is often helpful for getting unstuck. Organizations can use facilitators to help them address deeper issues; spiritual directors and counselors can help individuals.

Another helpful idea for getting unstuck is to try an incremental experiment. Do some small things to get moving, actions that move in a certain direction without committing you to it. For example, if you want a new job but never do anything about it, you might try some job-search experiments to see what happens. Call five friends, tell them you are looking for a job, and ask them for the names of people you could talk to. Follow up on the contacts. If you are invited to interview, do so.

Calling this an experiment means that you are just testing the waters. It's not a decision; you are trying things out. The idea is to have some experiences that you can reflect on and learn from.

A Good Decision Is Made in Freedom

Most of the work we do in decision making is the struggle to be free. Outwardly, we might seem to be among the freest people who have ever lived. Inwardly, we are afflicted with what Ignatius called disordered attachments. We are fearful and anxious, focused on ourselves, full of unruly desires; our heads are stuffed with shoulds and musts that come from our culture, other people, and sinister spiritual forces. We are equipped with a great capacity to rationalize these dubious attachments. We admit to some challenges, but we're basically okay.

Recall Ignatius's parable of the three types of men, which we discussed earlier. To recap: three spiritually sensitive men have each won a fortune in the lottery. Each is alert to the dangers that the money presents. Each wants to use the money as God would have him use it.

The first man is "all talk and no action." He talks about being free of the money, but he does nothing about it. The second man devises some uses for the money. He may start a business, set up a foundation to support some good work, or even give some of the money away. But these are his own plans that he wants God to ratify. He wants to do good on his own terms.

The third man seeks to be completely detached from the money. He desires neither to keep his fortune nor to get rid of it. He wants to be perfectly free to do with it what God wants to do with it. Achieving this degree of detachment is difficult. In a sense, it's easier to simply give the money away than it is to be so perfectly detached that you would do anything with it, as long as God wants it.

This parable helps us put the finger on the ways we deceive ourselves. It's easier to imagine ourselves being open than it is to actually *be* open. There's a little bit of the all talk and no action person in each of us. There's probably even more of the second person in us—the one who wants to be free on his or her own terms. This exercise helps bring our nonnegotiables to the surface. What assumptions underlie our thinking as we look at our choices? What vision of the good life do we hold to? What dream have we been pursuing? The point is not necessarily to put these things aside but to become aware of the hold they have on us so that we can be free to choose as God would have us choose.

We will encounter fears as we probe the nonnegotiables. *I'm afraid to do this because my spouse won't like it . . . I might fail at that job . . . The grad school might turn me down . . . I'll have to take a pay cut . . . My friends will think I'm crazy . . . I'm comfortable with my life the way it is.*

Here are a couple of steps you can take to face your fears:

- *Be honest.* Admit to yourself and to God that attachments to ideas and values are preventing you from being truly free. Name them. Recognize that you are not ready to make a decision until they are dealt with.
- *Act as if you were free.* Make a sincere effort to consider your alternatives freely, as if you were not attached to one or the other. Think about what it would be like not to have the attachments you have. Tell God that you want to follow his desires, even if you only want to want that.
- *Pray to be free.* Ask God for the gift of freedom. If you are strongly attracted to one alternative, pray to be ready to accept the other.

Approach the search for freedom with humility and realism. Ultimately, freedom is a gift from God; we can't achieve it on our own. We also must face the fact that we will never be perfectly free. Even if we could achieve perfect freedom, we would never know it for sure. We are flawed human beings who have spent years erecting and fortifying our nonnegotiables. God can release us from attachments, but in this life, we will never be sure that we are no longer encumbered by them.

A Good Decision Is Balanced and Involves the Whole Person

A sound decision is balanced. It is like a stool that rests solidly on three legs. It is in touch with God and holy revelation; it is in touch with the inner movements of the heart; it is in touch with the external world. If one of these legs is weak or missing, the stool becomes shaky. Something important has been overlooked.

Many people stand on one leg. Some are exquisitely attuned to their inner lives. They pray a lot, monitor and interpret their feelings, and spend time in contemplation and reflection. But they are not so alert to life in the real world. We say they have their heads in the clouds.

Others are men and women of action. They are quite in touch with events in the world. They read the signs of the times and eagerly set out to change the way things are. But they will get in trouble if they are not adequately in touch with their feelings and the feelings of others.

We've also met people who are spiritual but not religious. They are sensitive to the unseen world of the spirit, but their discernment is not anchored in a definitive revelation of God that carries authority. They run a great risk of confusing their own preferences and desires with the will of God.

The sociologist Christian Smith calls this moralistic therapeutic deism. It is a creed that rests on five tenets: (1) there is a God who created and ordered the world and watches over human life on the earth; (2) this God wants people to be good, nice, and fair to one another, as taught in the Bible and by religions throughout the world; (3) the central goal of life is to be happy and to feel good about oneself; (4) God does not need to be particularly involved in one's life except when needed to resolve a problem; and (5) all other theological and ethical statements are relative, which is true primarily if they work for you.

Moralistic therapeutic deism is not the historical Christian faith. For that matter, it's not consistent with any of the great religions of the world. It's an assertion of the freedom of the individual to do whatever seems good. The problem is that our perception of the good is obscured by our prejudices, wishful thinking, and unruly desires—this perception changes constantly. Different things appeal to different parts of our divided selves. What seems good for my career isn't so good for my family. A project that seems worthwhile requires more time and effort than I'm willing to give. What looked like fun yesterday looks like a waste of time today.

A good decision brings wholeness. It brings the parts of the divided self into balance.

A Good Decision Is a Spiral into Deeper Knowledge

A good decision usually takes us to places we don't expect. The process is not always orderly, and it can involve 180-degree turns. We can wind up making a choice that wasn't even on the table when we began. Most of the time, the process of making an important decision doesn't unfold the way we thought it would. It bears repeating: the process is a spiral rather than a straight line from point A to point B.

Dan is a fifty-five-year-old information technology manager who has been without full-time employment for two years. He has been making a decent living as a consultant, but he dislikes the uncertainty of the consultant's life. He wants a full-time permanent job.

Two job offers come Dan's way, but they're not dream jobs. One would require him to work in the company's Beijing office for two weeks every month. The other is a very difficult job with a company with serious management problems and a very uncertain future. Dan does not want to be away from his family half the time. Nor does he want to take on a job that he might not be able to perform successfully. Nevertheless, he sets out to make a decision about which job to accept.

Dan doesn't receive a clear answer. Instead, he gets more questions. Why does he feel impelled to take a highly unsatisfactory job? Is the security of a regular paycheck more important than job satisfaction and being with his family? In fact, why does he want a permanent job at all? What's wrong with continuing as a consultant?

Dan finds elements of fear, pride, and insecurity in his attitude. The uncertainty of a consultant's life makes him worry that he won't find enough work (even though he always has). This anxiety betrays a lack of confidence in his own skills. He also realizes that he is drawn to an important job with a big

company because that would make him feel good
about himself and look good in the eyes of others.

It might seem as if Dan is going backward in his decision
making rather than forward. He revisits old questions, but
he is not going backward. He is going deeper. He is learning something about himself; he is being invited to personal
growth. He is seeing that he need not be driven by fears,
pride, and anxiety when he thinks about work. To go even
deeper, Dan might stop praying for a permanent job and start
praying for wisdom about why he is so anxious about work. A
prayer like that opens up the possibility of discernment, and
discernment is at the heart of Ignatian decision making.

Dan's experience illustrates the spiral quality of Ignatian
discernment. His decision-making process is not a straight
line. He reflects on his experience and moves to a decision;
then he reconsiders his experience in a new and deeper way.
If Dan were just rehashing the same thought process over
and over, he would appear to be going in circles. But he's not
doing that. He is going deeper as he gains insight. His trajec-
tory is a spiral, not an endless circle.

Even comparing discernment to a spiral can be misleading. In real life, decision making often proceeds in a course
full of surprises, zigs and zags, and U-turns. That's the way
it should be. *The goal of discernment is not to get to some final*
destination as efficiently as possible, but to continue to go deeper
and deeper into our relationship with God.

Dan might have had to learn this in the process of his
prayer. For instance, his first prayers might have been driven
by a sense that God was very demanding. This would have
reinforced his fears and insecurities. That image of God
might have led him to believe that he needed to get a real

job! Dan might have needed outside input to realize that the real God would not treat him like this. He could have gotten this input from a spiritual guide or from reading Scripture or seeing an inspirational movie. Any of these sources might have helped him to imagine the God whom Ignatius came to know. The one who labors for us and who "works all things for good" (Romans 8:28).

As we have been saying, all he really needed to recognize the voice of the real God was a sincere desire to choose the good and to grow in love. That is the one thing necessary. All else will fall into place if this is what we truly seek. Even choices that seem to be mistakes are part of the spiral. The main thing isn't the decision. It's moving along the path of love and service.

A Final Word

Times when we are faced with important decisions are times of great opportunity, but they can also be times of great anxiety. Decision making is inherently troublesome. We can never know for sure where certain choices will lead us. We can never be sure we have all the data. We cannot even be sure that the so-called facts we have are true or that we understand these facts correctly.

At such times, any tools that help us come to some clarity and guide us through the decision-making process are quite a gift. And as far as this kind of gift goes, Ignatius' tools for decision making represent a veritable treasure.

When it seems that we are awash in a sea of confusing emotions, Ignatian tools help us to sort through these emotions. When we feel like our emotions are pulling us in one direction and our thoughts pull us in another, Ignatius helps us bring our thoughts and emotions into harmony. He helps us work from our heart where emotions, thoughts, and gut instincts come together.

Anyone who has made an important decision can tell you that having a clear sense of your own identity can make the decision-making process much easier. And as we have seen, Ignatius' methods help us to know our true selves better.

What's more, Ignatius's guidelines help us to understand who God is. They help us see how God leads us by sending consolation. This consolation, in turn, can guide us to a place of lasting peace. It is a place that feels like home, because in many ways it *is* our true home.

We wrote this book, to share these bits of Ignatian wisdom with you We do not strive to remove all uncertainty from the decision-making process. We know that is impossible. What *is* possible, with Ignatius' help, is to learn to see the decision-making process as an opportunity. Specifically, it is an opportunity to grow in self knowledge and to grow in our relationship with God. We have seen this in our own experience. As we come to know our true selves, and the true God, we come to know of a love that is patient, a love that is kind, one that "is not jealous, is not pompous, it is not inflated, it is not rude, it does not seek its own interests, it is not quick-tempered, it does not brood over injury, it does not rejoice over wrongdoing but rejoices with the truth. It bears all things, believes all things, hopes all things, endures all things." (1 Corinthians 13:4–7).

And so it is, not out of a sense of fear, but rather with great hope that we pose this question to you: What is your decision?

Handy Reference:
How the Rules of
Discernment Help Us
Make Good Decisions

A handful of themes run through Ignatius's twenty-two rules for discernment of spirits. Here's a summary of twelve principles that are especially useful for decision making.

- *The shifting feelings you have when you contemplate a decision have meaning.* They are clues as to the right direction to go in.

- *Don't make a decision when you're feeling desperate, anxious, pressured, or otherwise distressed.* You'll be tempted to act because you want the bad feelings to go away. Don't. Wait until tranquility returns.

- *Talk to someone.* A sure sign of the work of the evil spirit is the urge to keep important developments secret and to make important decisions by yourself.

- *Be patient.* Especially when you've become anxious about how long a decision is taking and others are urging you to act. (However, some decisions have time limits on them—do the best you can.)

- *Know your weaknesses with regard to making decisions.* Are you impulsive? Do you procrastinate? Are you overly proud? These tendencies are where you are likely to run into trouble.

- *Disruptive feelings are likely to be subtle.* Desolation will come in the form of doubts and worries hidden in spiritual language: "Maybe I should do that hard and unappealing thing because God wants me to."

- *Be careful about cloaking your personal interest in spiritual language.* Most of us can readily assure ourselves that what we want is what God wants.

- *What's the feeling of the feeling?* The Holy Spirit is gentle and affirming. The evil spirit is noisy and disruptive.

- *Keep reviewing your thoughts and actions and motives.* Growing in the ability to make good decisions takes time and is a thoughtful, probing process. If we spend time in this way, we will eventually be able recognize a real qualitative difference between the actions of the good and evil spirits.

- *The relationship with God is the thing.* It's okay to make mistakes. Decisions lead to more decisions but also to a deeper sense of our true selves and an easier recognition of the true God.

- *The work of the enemy is likely to be subtle.* We will seldom be tempted to do something that's obviously wrong. Instead, the wrong path will appear to be something good.

- *Talk to a wise adviser.* We need help sorting through the subtle movements of spirits.

See www.ignatianspirituality.com/making-good-decisions for more information about discernment and making choices.

Handy Reference:
The Three Approaches
to Making Decisions

BEFORE MAKING A DECISION

Pray for the light to make the best decision.
Pray to know God's will.
Pray for freedom to be open to the options available.

MODE 1: "NO DOUBT ABOUT IT"
(CHAPTER 9)

God makes it unmistakably clear that a certain choice is
the correct one. It is usually a sudden peak experience,
but certainty can also emerge gradually. The discernment process consists of assessing the genuineness of the
experience.

MODE 2: DISCERNING SPIRITUAL MOVEMENTS (CHAPTER 10)

1. Pray for knowledge of God's will.

2. Pray for freedom.

3. Notice movements of consolation and desolation.

4. Imagine yourself having made the decision: Try an option on for size! Be aware of consolations and desolations in this decision.

5. Try the other option on for size. Note consolations and desolations.

6. Discern the source and direction of these feelings. Are they from the good spirit or the evil spirit?

7. What does this mean for your decision?

8. Discuss it with someone.

9. Decide and seek confirmation of the decision.

MODE 3: CALM DELIBERATION (CHAPTER 11)

1. Identify the decision to be made.
   - The issue should be practical and real.
   - The decision should be one that you have the right to make.

- You must have the information to make an intelligent decision.

2. State the choice concretely.

3. Pray for inner freedom.

4. Gather all the necessary information.

5. Pray for inner freedom, again.

6. Make a list of advantages and disadvantages.

7. Evaluate the advantages and disadvantages.
   - Which reasons seem to be the most important?
   - What core values emerge?
   - Which core values seem more consistent with your true self?

8. Test your reasoning with your imagination.

9. Make a tentative decision.

10. Confirm the decision.

11. Make your decision even if you are not certain about it.

See www.ignatianspirituality.com/making-good-decisions for more information about discernment and making choices.

Acknowledgments

This book grew out of a daylong workshop on Ignatian decision making that Tim Hipskind and Michael Sparough gave at Loyola University Chicago. Both had given presentations of this material on their own previously, but this marked their first attempt at blending very different approaches to teaching Ignatian decision making. The result was a hit! Tim and Michael knew that they had come up with an approach that was significantly stronger than either of them could have done by himself.

Joe Durepos, Matthew Diener, and Jim Manney at Loyola Press had the idea of turning this material into a book. Jim joined our writing team and guided us through the lengthy process of making a workshop transcript into a substantial book. The final product is a true collaboration among the three of us.

The original presentation was a joint effort between the Institute of Pastoral Studies and Charis Ministries, a Jesuit outreach to adults in their twenties and thirties. Sister Mary George Boklage, RSM and Nancy Kern from Heart to Heart, a small publisher based in Cincinnati, had the foresight to record the talks. Ranell Sleman from Charis transcribed those recordings with patient care. We are most grateful to Heart to Heart and Charis Ministries for providing the initial seed money to capture the teachings of that workshop. Were it not for their help, this book would not exist.

We are especially grateful to Bill Creed, SJ, Bill Barry, SJ and Bernie Owens, SJ. These exceptional teachers of the *Spiritual Exercises* read the manuscript with great care and offered constructive suggestions on a very tight timeline. We are much honored to have the help of these men who have taught us so much of what we write about.

We are grateful as well to other teachers, mentors, and spiritual directors. From these we have learned a great deal about discernment by virtue of their wisdom and their example.

Vinita Wright, our editor, is to be thanked for helping us to further clarify our thought and Katherine Faydash for her great attention to detail in the copyediting.

Finally, we thank all those who allowed us to tell their stories in this book. Many of the illustrations we used are based on real life discernments from people we have known in more than forty years of working in ministry. Their stories give us courage to believe that even in making less than perfect decisions, the good spirit will help us find our way to much joy and peace!

J. Michael Sparough, SJ
Jim Manney
Tim Hipskind, SJ

November 5, 2009
Feast of the Saints and Blessed
of the Society of Jesus